UNEMPLOYMENT and INFLATION

THE NEW ECONOMICS OF THE WAGE-PRICE SPIRAL

ROGER LeROY MILLER
Department of Economics
University of Washington

RABURN M. WILLIAMS
College of Business Administration
University of Hawaii

WEST PUBLISHING CO.
St. Paul • New York • Boston
Los Angeles • San Francisco

132972

COPYRIGHT © 1974 By WEST PUBLISHING CO.
All rights reserved
Printed in the United States of America
Library of Congress Cataloging in Publication Data

Miller, Roger LeRoy.
    Unemployment and inflation.

    1. Wage-price policy. 2. Inflation (Finance). 3. Unemployed.
I. Williams, Raburn M., joint author. II. Title.
HC79.W24M54   331.2'1'01   74–1062
ISBN 0–8299–0009–8

    Miller & Williams–Unemploy. & Inflat. WCB
    1st Reprint—1975

PREFACE

The problems of unemployment and inflation are still with us today. The simplified text book analysis that was so prevalent for the past 25 years has not, as everyone well knows, been successful in explaining the simultaneous occurrence of these two economic "bads." Moreover, the lack of understanding of how unemployment and inflation could simultaneously occur has perhaps prompted policy makers to too hastily attempt direct controls over the behavior of economic agents.

It is our hope that this small monograph will allow concerned professional economists as well as students to have a better understanding of microeconomic theory, which can help explain many of the pressing dilemmas facing the United States today (and the rest of the world, for that matter).

This book is aimed at concerned professional economists as well as students of macroeconomics, monetary theory, and, to a lesser extent, labor economics. Although we do use some probability theory, the reader can still obtain a good understanding of the economic theories we do present without actually dwelling on the equations.

A few years back, some economists were claiming that macroeconomics was intellectually moribund. We do not think that to be true, and we hope that the reader will agree with us.

ROGER LeROY MILLER
Seattle, Washington
RABURN M. WILLIAMS
Honolulu, Hawaii

February, 1974

*

TABLE OF CONTENTS

Chapter		Page
1. INTRODUCTION		1
2. SUPPLY, DEMAND AND THE TWO TYPES OF INFLATION		5
	I. Introduction	5
	II. Aggregate Demand and the Circular Flow of Income	5
	A. The Government Budget Constraint	7
	B. Taxation by Inflation	8
	III. A Model of Determinants of the Money Supply	9
	IV. Income Flows and Money Creation	10
	V. Balancing Leakages	12
	VI. Interest Rates and the Velocity of Money	13
	VII. A Recap	18
	VIII. Determinants of Aggregate Supply and the Demand for Labor	19
	A. A Cobb-Douglas Production Function Example	21
	B. Empirical Evidence	22
	C. Cyclical Fluctuations	22
	IX. Putting Supply and Demand Together	23
	X. Inflation: Demand-Pull and Cost-Push	24
	XI. Weaknesses in the Above Two Models	26
3. A THEORY OF INVESTMENT IN UNEMPLOYMENT		28
	I. Introduction	28
	II. Unemployment	29
	A. Search Unemployment	30
	III. The Reservation Wage Rate	31
	A. Finding the Reservation Wage	34
	IV. The Duration of Unemployment	34
	A. Where the Variance of the Probability Density Function is Zero	37
	B. Variance of Probability Density Function is Greater Than Zero	38

TABLE OF CONTENTS

Chapter		Page
3.	A THEORY OF INVESTMENT IN UNEMPLOYMENT—Continued	
	V. Search Unemployment and Errors in Forecasting	40
	A. Specification of the Relationship	42
	B. The Friedman Theory of the Phillips Curve Relationship	44
	C. Institutional Considerations	44
4.	THE TRADE-OFF BETWEEN UNEMPLOYMENT AND INFLATION	46
	I. Introduction	46
	II. The United States' Empirical Relationship	50
	III. Expectations and the Phillips Curve	54
	IV. Introducing Changing Expectations	56
5.	THE FORMATION OF EXPECTATIONS	59
	I. Irving Fisher's Research on Expectations Formation	59
	II. Recent Developments in Adaptive Expectations Models	60
	III. Further Justification of Adaptive Expectations Model	61
	IV. Other Versions of the Model	63
	V. Using a Model to Form Expectations	65
	VI. Direct Controls	65
6.	THE EMPLOYMENT AND PRICE EFFECTS OF LABOR MARKET RESTRICTIONS	66
	I. Union Collective Bargaining	67
	II. Demand for Labor	69
	A. Derived Demand for Labor When Capital Supply is Perfectly Elastic	73
	B. Demand for Labor When Capital Supply is Perfectly Inelastic	73
	C. The More General Case	74
	III. Empirical Examples of the Derived Demand for Labor	75
	IV. Employer Collusion	76
	V. Welfare Effects of Wage Differentials	78
	VI. General Equilibrium Considerations	80
	A. A Two Sector General Equilibrium Model of Union Wage Policies	81

TABLE OF CONTENTS

Chapter

6. THE EMPLOYMENT AND PRICE EFFECTS OF LABOR MARKET RESTRICTIONS—Continued

		Page
VII.	Minimum Wage Rates, Collective Bargaining and Southern Industrial Development	83
	A. Monopsony	86
VIII.	Aggregate Demand and Labor Market Restriction	88

7. WAGE AND PRICE CONTROLS ... 91
   - I. Expectations ... 92
   - II. Aggregate Excess Demand Situations ... 93
     - A. Macro Considerations ... 94
     - B. Micro Considerations ... 94
     - C. Inventories ... 98
   - III. Price Searchers Market ... 98
   - IV. Fixed and Variable Cost Considerations ... 102
   - V. Effects of Alternative Control Schemes ... 103
   - VI. Conclusions ... 105

8. POLICY-MAKING IN THE POST-NEW ECONOMIC ERA ... 106

Index ... 109

†

UNEMPLOYMENT AND INFLATION:
THE NEW ECONOMICS OF THE
WAGE-PRICE SPIRAL

CHAPTER 1. INTRODUCTION

Full employment and stable prices have been the two principal goals of economic policy since the Employment Act of 1946. Until the late 1950s, policy makers seldom questioned the compatibility of these goals since aggregate demand policies were generally considered to be independent of aggregate supply conditions. The latter were typically analyzed in terms of exogenous (principally institutional) factors such as the institutional setting of wage rates in the organized sectors of the economy. Theories of continued "creeping inflation" were based on the presumed attempt by organized labor to increase its share of national income.

Wage increases in excess of increases in worker productivity were considered the heart of the inflation problem. This concern for cost-push inflation eventually produced numerical government guidelines to exert restraint on wages to eliminate inflation. Every *Economic Report of the President and the Council of Economic Advisors* since 1957 has stressed, in one form or another, that private pricing discretion should be tempered to create stable prices. Restraint on the part of business and workers has been requested. The 1960 *Economic Report* was explicit in stating that wage increases should not exceed the growth in average *national* productivity. It further suggested that price reductions were called for in sectors experiencing exceptionally rapid productivity growth. The 1962 *Report* gave a formal statement of guideposts for wage increases: they should not exceed 3.2 percent.

Aggregate demand policies were independently designed to produce full employment. The explicit use of the government budget and monetary policy to attain a specific unemployment rate goal was believed possible because of the assumption of an exogenous price level. The policies of the New Economists were accepted in an atmosphere of expected price stability. Expansionary monetary and fiscal policies were sold to the President and also to the American people; deficit spending was to be the key to prosperity.

However, at the same time some economists (Phillips in England and Samuelson and Solow here in the United States) suggested the existence of a trade-off between inflation and unemployment. This analysis implied that lower unemployment rates could be attained only at the cost of a higher rate of inflation. Beginning with our increased involvement in Indochina in 1965, this apparent policy dilemma increasingly preoccupied the minds of economic policy-makers. The political success of expansionary monetary and fiscal policies during the Kennedy and early Johnson administrations quickly gave way to distress about accelerating inflation.

The deteriorating trade-off between inflation and unemployment produced new developments in economic analysis. It soon became apparent that a higher rate of inflation might only be capable of temporarily reducing the level of unemployment. If this so-called accelerationist theory is correct, subnormal unemployment rates could be permanently maintained only by accelerating the rate of inflation in an *unanticipated* manner. If the accelerationists are correct, the employment justification for aggregate demand policies is seriously undermined.

Some economists still maintain that the worsening trade-off between inflation and unemployment is due to institutional factors such as increased market power of organized labor and monopoly producers. However, institutional factors can affect the attainable combination of unemployment and inflation for only short periods of time. In the long run, institutional factors determine *relative* prices, not *absolute* prices. Increases in union wages due to collective bargaining agreements may reduce nonunion wages. Institutional labor market restrictions may have their principal effect on the structure of wages rather than on their absolute level. Similarly, monopolists who restrict output in order to raise prices also release resources which can increase output and lower prices elsewhere in the economy. Market power determines relative prices, not absolute prices.

Concern for the deteriorating trade-off between inflation and unemployment led policy makers to impose the August 15, 1971 freeze on wages and prices. With this bold economic measure, policy makers created a new tool to independently control aggregate supply conditions.

These new economic approaches to the unemployment-inflation dilemma also raises the question: "What is the optimal unemployment rate?" In the pursuit of low unemployment goals, policy-makers must realize that a certain amount of unemployment is voluntary. Indeed, the movement of workers from low productivity to high productivity sectors of the economy usually involves some period of unemployment. Such unemployment contributes to economic growth which raises real wage rates.

In this book we shall develop economic paradigms which illustrate the dimensions of the inflation-unemployment problem. In the process, we present a simplified aggregate demand and supply model which is used to describe the two forms of inflation: demand-pull and cost-push. Both concepts are obtained by making either absolute prices or output exogenous. Alternatively, a model of search unemployment can be used to derive output conditions in terms of expectation of inflation. We do this in a following chapter on "A Theory of Investment in Unemployment." The search unemployment model casts doubt on the social desirability of certain "naive" low unemployment rate goals.

The important role of price expectations in causing fluctuations in the unemployment rate around its "long-run normal" level is linked to the Phillips curve analysis in Chapter 4. If expectations of inflation are unbiased in the long-run, there can be no permanent trade-off between inflation and unemployment. In Chapter 5 the Phillips curve relationship is discussed in terms of models of price expectation formulation which assume rational behavior by economic agents.

Since institutional factors enter frequently into the analysis of the unemployment problem, we present certain aspects of microeconomic labor theory. More specifically, the derived demand is developed in the context of labor market restriction—unions, minimum wages, etc. This analysis deals with the theory of *relative* prices, not necessarily *absolute* prices. In that sense, it departs from the macroeconomic context of the previous chapters.

The next to last chapter treats the economics of wage and price controls. There we consider the costs as well as the presumed benefits of price controlled markets.

Finally, we comment on policy-making in the Post-New Economic Era. We predict that economic policies based on the presumption of a stable law of disequilibrium price dynamics are certain to fail.

CHAPTER 2. SUPPLY, DEMAND AND THE TWO TYPES OF INFLATION

I. INTRODUCTION

The basic framework for understanding inflation, unemployment, and stabilization policies can be derived from the simple determinants of aggregate demand and supply and the interrelationship of these two functions. While we do not provide a definitive examination of aggregate demand and supply, these essential relationships are sufficient to allow an analysis of inflation and unemployment. The model will assume a closed economy. We treat the demand side of the question in a manner which focuses attention on the importance of government expenditures and how they are financed. In order to do this, we shall develop the elements of aggregate demand in terms of an extremely simplified liquidity preference function.

In developing the supply side of the analysis, we rely principally on the assumption of profit maximization with an aggregate Cobb-Douglas production function. This aggregate demand and supply model can be used to illustrate the demand-pull and cost-push versions of inflation. We will see, however, that the resultant models of both types of inflation have related weaknesses which are resolved in a subsequent chapter on the Phillips curve relationship between inflation and unemployment.

II. AGGREGATE DEMAND AND THE CIRCULAR FLOW OF INCOME

The concept of aggregate *nominal* demand (total spending expressed in current dollars) is derived from the basic circular flow of income. The circular flow of money (or nominal) income follows from the fact that income received by individuals is derived from the sale of goods and services and provides the principal source of funds for GNP expenditures. A rise in the price level at full employment would automatically increase income, providing the additional funds to purchase the full employment output at the higher price level. The determination of the *absolute* price level at which full employment output can be sold must be derived by balancing the supply of funds in addition to income that can be used to finance GNP expenditures against net leakage from the circular flow of income.

In analyzing the circular flow of income from the supply of funds point of view, credit plays an important role in financing expenditures. Approximately 40 to 60% of GNP expenditures are financed with borrowed funds. Most of these borrowed funds, however, represent a mere transfer between individuals; they do not represent an additional source of funds for GNP expenditures. It is only the *net* loans to the private sector from either the government sector (which includes the central bank) or the commercial banking system which can provide a source of funds for GNP expenditures in addition to income generated by the sale of goods and services. The determination of the absolute price level at which full employment output can be sold is derived by balancing any additional sources of funds against net leakages from the circular flow of income.

There is one major source of leakage from the circular flow of income, hoarding. Hoarding consists of increases in the desired holdings of currency or demand deposits. Hoarding can only occur when an individual's expenditures are less than the receipts he acquires through the sale of goods, services, or assets. It is important to note that hoarding is the only form of saving which does not flow into GNP expenditures. To obtain a more meaningful definition of hoarding, we must look at the basic budget constraint facing the private, nonbanking sector of the economy. Whereas for an individual hoarding occurs whenever expenditures are less than receipts, for the entire private nonbanking sector of the economy:

$$\text{Hoarding} = Y - T - \triangle B + \triangle L - E^d \qquad (2\text{--}1)$$

where Y = income

T = taxes

$\triangle B$ = net borrowing on the part of the government from the private sector

$\triangle L$ = net borrowing from the commercial banks by the private sector

E^d = desired private expenditures on goods and services.

In a closed economy, equilibrium in the goods and services market requires that desired expenditures equal income because income is the total receipts from the sale of output. This leads us to a basic equilibrium accounting relation which holds *ex ante* only in equilibrium, but always *ex post* if the word "actual" is substituted for the word "desired."

$$Y = E^d + G \qquad (2\text{-}2)$$

where G = government expenditures

E^d = desired consumption expenditures + desired investment expenditures

Both desired consumption and investment expenditures are already included in equation 2-1, the budget constraint of the private nonbanking sector. However, the government itself (including the central bank) faces a budget constraint which cannot be ignored when considering the effects of government stabilization policies.

A. THE GOVERNMENT BUDGET CONSTRAINT

The most obvious forms of finance for government activities are taxes and net borrowing from the private sector. In order to understand the way in which the government finances its expenditures, we must start with the government budget constraint. Government expenditures must be equal to net borrowing, taxes, and the creation of high-powered money:

$$\triangle H = G - T - \triangle B \qquad (2\text{-}3)$$

where $\triangle H$ = changes in high-powered money or the monetary base

Part of the income flows in the economy are generated by government expenditures. However, those government expenditures which are financed either by taxes or net borrowing from the private sector automatically reduce the funds available for private sector expenditures in total GNP. In other words, government expenditures financed by taxes or net borrowing take out of the circular flow of income funds that the private sector otherwise may have used for GNP expenditures. In order to focus on this fact, we go back to the individual budget constraint facing the private, nonbanking sector. If the demand for money remains constant, i. e., there is no hoarding or dishoarding, taxes or net lending to the government necessarily reduce desired private expenditures on goods and services. Given this assumption, an increase in government expenditures financed by an increase in taxes or net borrowing by the government from the private sector is fully offset by a reduction in private expenditures. More formally, we can reformulate the equilibrium accounting identity 2–2 as:

$$G = Y - E^d \qquad (2\text{–}4)$$

In other words, in ex ante equilibrium, government expenditures on goods and services are equal to the gap between actual income, Y, and desired expenditures on the part of the private sector, E^d. This equilibrium gap is created either by tax payments or net borrowing by the government from the private sector, for both tax payments and net borrowing reduce the funds available for GNP expenditures by the private sector.

B. TAXATION BY INFLATION

However, as Keynes once said, "A government can live for a long time, even the German government or the Russian government, by printing paper money."[1] Keynes realized that governments could in effect tax another way—by inflation. This method of taxation is similar to direct taxes as we normally know them in that it also creates the gap between actual income and desired private expenditures necessary to finance real government expenditures. In order to simplify the flow of funds analysis, we shall consolidate the Treasury with the Federal Reserve System. In this manner we can derive actual changes in high-powered money or the monetary base. High-powered money consists of the monetary liabilities of the Federal Reserve System or of the United States Treasury. These liabilities are used as currency in the hands of the public or as commercial banks' reserves which must be held against their deposits. The relationship between changes in the monetary base and the total money supply can be derived from the following simple model of the determinants of money in circulation.

---

1. Keynes, J. M., *A Tract on Monetary Reform*, Macmillan, London, 1923, p. 37.

III. A MODEL OF DETERMINANTS OF THE MONEY SUPPLY

The simplest model of the determination of the money supply relates that stock, M, to the stock of high-powered money, H.

$$M = \frac{M}{H} \cdot H \qquad (2\text{--}5)$$

The ratio $\frac{M}{H}$ is usually called the money supply multiplier.

For expositional simplicity, the money supply will be defined here as demand deposits (D) plus currency (C).

$$M = C + D \qquad (2\text{--}6)$$

The stock of high-powered money can be used either as currency in the hands of the nonbanking public (C) or as reserves of the commercial banking system (R).

$$H = C + R \qquad (2\text{--}7)$$

In our fractional reserve banking system, the reserves (R) are held against both demand and time deposit liabilities. The reserve requirements differ for these two types of commercial bank liabilities, hence:

$$R = r_d D + r_t T \qquad (2\text{--}8)$$

where r_d and r_t are the reserve ratios held against demand and time deposit liabilities, respectively.

Now if we substitute 2–6 and 2–7 into 2–5, then further substitute 2–8 into 2–7, we obtain:

$$M = \frac{M}{H} H = \frac{C+D}{C+R} H = \frac{1 + \frac{C}{D}}{\frac{C}{D} + r_d + r_t \frac{T}{D}} H \qquad (2\text{--}9)$$

Hence, the size of the money supply multiplier depends upon:
1. The form in which the nonbanking public desires to hold its money (cash balances).
2. The reserve ratios that commercial banks desire to hold against their demand and time deposit liabilities.

IV. INCOME FLOWS AND MONEY CREATION

Increases in the money supply are an important source of funds for GNP expenditures in addition to income derived from the sale of goods and services. Bank deposits other than demand deposits are not included in the money supply as defined here. They are merely regarded here as loans within the private sector with banks acting as intermediaries. A change in the supply of money can be broken down into changes in the monetary base and net borrowing from the commercial banking sector by the private, nonbanking sector ($\triangle L$).

$$\text{Changes in the money supply} = \triangle H + \triangle L \qquad (2\text{--}10)$$

We can now rewrite the budget constraint for the private, nonbanking sector (2–1) as:

$$\text{Hoarding} = Y - T - \triangle B + \triangle L + G - (E^d + G) \qquad (2\text{--}11)$$

Since we know by 2–3 that

$$\triangle H = G - T - \triangle B \qquad (2\text{--}12)$$

the specification of the propensity to hoard, 2–11, becomes:

$$\text{Hoarding} = \triangle M^d = Y + \triangle M^s - (E^d + G) \qquad (2\text{--}13)$$

This consolidation follows from 2–10 and 2–12 above.

If we look at the hoarding function in form 2–13, the monetary nature of the equilibrium level of nominal or money aggregate demand is clearly revealed. Let us look at the static equilibrium case where $\triangle M^s = 0$, that is, where the money supply remains constant. The equilibrium accounting identity requires that income minus private desired expenditures equal government expenditures, as we stated in equation 2–4. Hence, the demand for goods and services will only equal the supply of goods and services if hoarding is zero, that is, if the demand for money balances is equal to the supply of money balances. It is possible, then, to see why money creation is a means of creating the gap betwen actual output and desired private expenditures necessary to finance government expenditures.

When government spending is financed by money creation, the income available for spending by the private sector is not reduced as in the case of taxing or net borrowing. In a situation of full employment, increased government spending financed by money creation can only result in an inflation. This inflation, however, creates the necessary gap between total income and desired GNP expenditures by the private sector because it succeeds in reducing the purchasing power of nominal money or cash balances. This in turn induces individuals to desire larger nominal money balances. In other words, a reduction in the real value of money held causes hoarding to be positive. We note that the purchasing power of money balances depreciates at the rate of inflation. Hence, individuals who desire to maintain their real money balances must use some of their receipts to increase their nominal money balances at the inflationary rate. In the words of Keynes,

> Let us suppose that there are in circulation nine million currency notes, and that they have altogether a value equivalent to 36 million gold dollars. Suppose that the government prints a further three million notes, so that the amount of currency is now 12 million; then, in accordance with the above theory, the 12 million notes are still only equivalent to 36 million dollars. In the first state of affairs, therefore, each note = four dollars, and in the second state of affairs each note = three dollars. Consequently, the nine million notes originally held by the public are now worth 27 million dollars instead of 36 million dollars, and the three million notes newly issued by the government are worth nine million dollars. Thus by the process of printing the additional notes the government has transferred from the public to itself an amount of resources equal to nine million dollars just as successfully as if it had raised this sum in taxation.
>
> Keynes, A *Tract on Monetary Reform, op. cit.*, pp. 38–39.

It is obviously the portion of income that is used to increase nominal money balances which creates the gap between total output and desired private expenditures, the gap that is necessary to permit the government to bid goods and services away from the private sector. It is in this sense that inflation is a "tax" on money balances. The real resources which can be bid (or taxed) away from the private nonbanking sector by inflation is equal to the rate of inflation times the real money balances the private sector desires to maintain.[2] (We will always define real money balances as equal to M divided by P, where P is the price level.)

V. BALANCING LEAKAGES

Remember that in the beginning of this chapter we noted that the determination of the absolute price level at which full employment output can be sold is derived from the balancing of the supply of funds in addition to income that can be used to finance GNP expenditures against the net leakages from the circular flow of income. We now are able to see that balancing leakages from the expenditure stream against additional sources of funds for GNP expenditures is an alternative description of the monetary equilibrium which makes the demand and supply of money equal. To illustrate the monetary nature of the determination of total spending, we assume a simplified liquidity preference function, otherwise known as the Cambridge equation.

$$M^d = kyP \qquad (2\text{--}14)$$

where M^d = the demand for nominal cash balances

y = output (real income)

P = the price level

k = the ratio of desired money balances to nominal income (or the inverse of the income velocity of money)

---

[2]. The government does not receive all the proceeds of the inflationary "tax" on money balances since, in our fractional reserve system, the commercial banks participate in the growth of the money supply by expanding demand deposits. As a result, the commercial banking system receives part of the proceeds of the inflationary "tax" on money balances. Of course, if there were no prohibition of interest rates on demand deposits, competition among banks for depositors would force banks to return most of their share of the proceeds from inflation to depositors in the form of interest on deposits.

By using 2–14 we can derive the level of nominal income from the money supply by assuming that equilibrium requires money supplied to equal money demanded. As Keynes put it, ". . . incomes and . . . prices necessarily change until the aggregate of the amounts of money which individuals choose to hold at the new level of incomes and prices thus brought about has come to equality with the amount of money created by the banking system."[3]

A moving equilibrium situation would be described by the following equation:

$$\Delta \ln M^s - \Delta \ln k = \Delta \ln y + \Delta \ln P \qquad (2\text{--}15)$$

Note that nominal income can increase either by an increase in P or an increase in real output.

It is important to note that during the post-World War II period, there has been a distinguishable fall in the ratio of desired money balances to GNP. The secular reduction in k (increase in velocity) is usually attributed to changes in the payments mechanism or in market interest rates. In any event from 1960 to 1971 k declined at an average rate of about 2.5% per year. (See Figure 2–1.)

VI. INTEREST RATES AND THE VELOCITY OF MONEY

Even if the money supply remains constant (or, in a dynamic context, its growth rate is constant), other things can happen to affect nominal demand. For example, shifts in the demand and supply of loanable funds due to pure fiscal policy actions, new investment opportunities, or changing expectations of future rates of inflation may cause a change in interest rates. Although we have not specifically included the interest rate in our liquidity preference function 2–14, the interest rate obviously affects the demand for money because it is the opportunity cost of holding money if money earns no interest. More specifically, the opportunity cost of holding the currency component of the money supply is the nominal interest rate on alternative nonmonetary

---

3. *The General Theory of Employment, Interest and Money*, Macmillan, 1936, pp. 84–85.

assets, while the opportunity cost of holding the demand deposit component of money is the nominal interest rate on alternative nonmonetary assets minus the implicit rate of return paid on de-

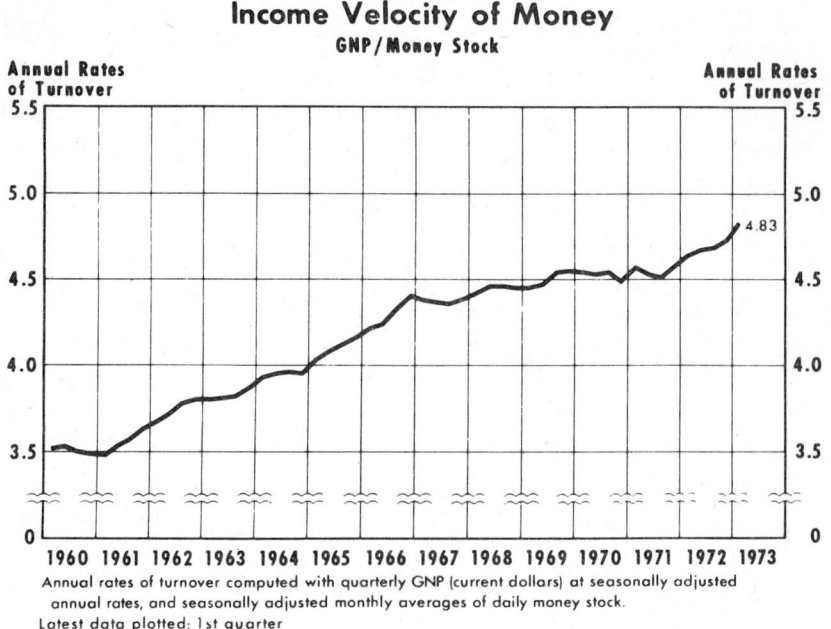

Figure 2-1

Secular change in velocity

mand deposits.[4] Individuals react to an increased opportunity cost of holding money by reducing their demand for money balances relative to nominal income. That is, they will reduce k. In fact, in the standard Hicksian IS–LM framework, this is the channel by which pure fiscal policy actions affect aggregate nominal demand. In the Hicksian framework pure fiscal policy actions leave the money supply unchanged.

---

4. Even though regulation Q prevents banks from paying interest on demand deposits, they do so by providing demand deposit holders with zero cost or below cost priced services.

We can see this more clearly by considering the following three-equation model:

$$C = f(y, i) \tag{2-16}$$

$$I = g(y, i) \tag{2-17}$$

$$\frac{M^d}{P} = h(y, i) \tag{2-18}$$

where C = consumption
   I = investment
   i = nominal interest rate

Equilibrium occurs when:

$$\frac{M^d}{P} = \frac{M^s}{P} \tag{2-19}$$

$$y = C + I + G \tag{2-20}$$

where G = real government expenditures (which are considered exogenous)

Equations 2-16 and 2-17 are used to derive the Hicksian IS schedule when constrained by 2-20. We note, however, that investment and consumption functions are correctly expressed in terms of the real interest rate. Consequently, this model holds only when the expected rate of inflation is constant. As a result of this assumption, any change in the nominal is also a change in the real rate of interest.

Equation 2-18, when constrained by equation 2-19, yields the Hicksian LM schedule. Any change in the price level will shift the LM schedule. Consequently, we can derive Figure 2-3, the relationship between P and y (the aggregate demand schedule), by obtaining the simultaneous solution of the IS and LM schedules. We graphically represent this in Figures 2-2 and 2-3.

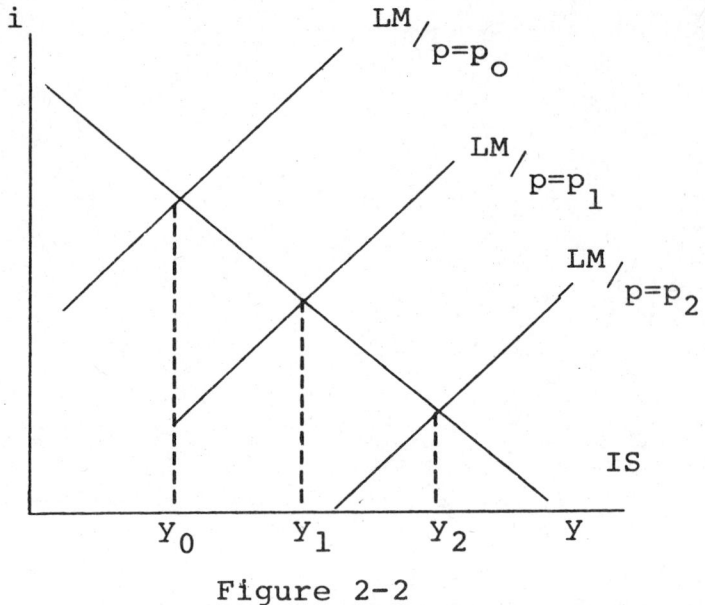

Figure 2-2

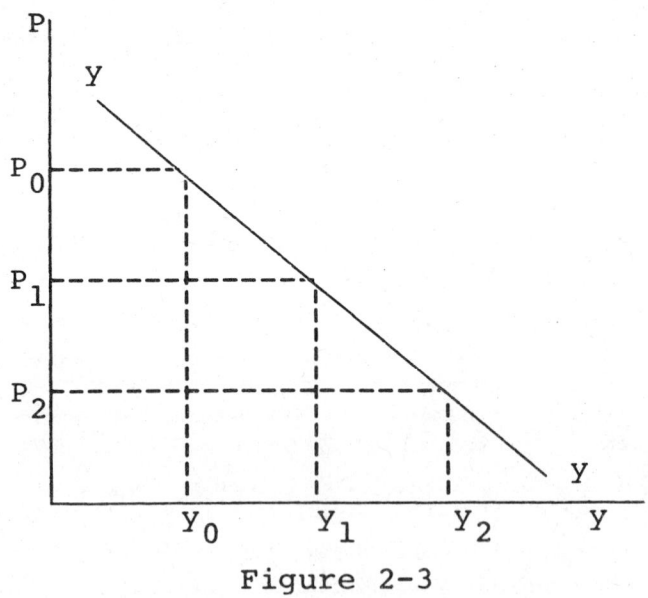

Figure 2-3

Any shift in the IS schedule which increases interest rates associated with a given level of real output shifts the aggregate demand associated with a given nominal money supply outward as indicated in Figures 2–4 and 2–5.

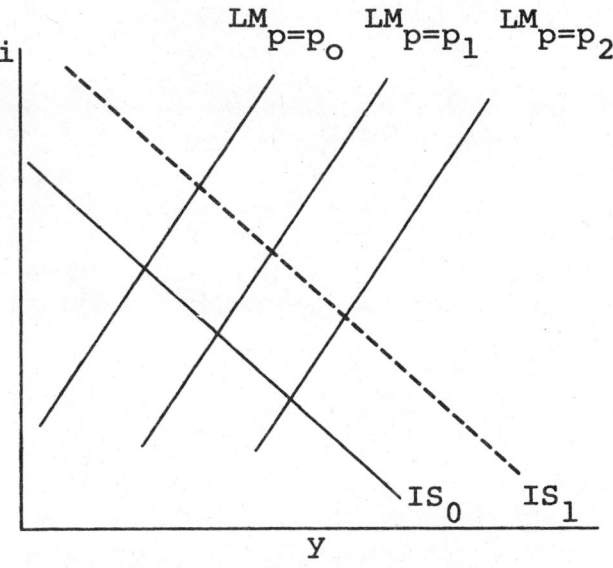

Figure 2-4

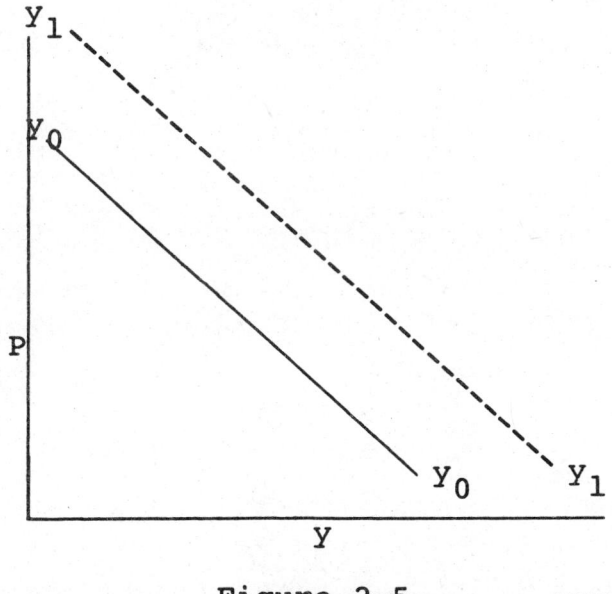

Figure 2-5

Note, however, that higher interest rates increase the revenue earned by banks on their demand deposit liabilities. If competition forces banks to pay increased implicit interest on demand deposits, higher market interest rates will also increase the implicit rate of return on demand deposit balances. An increase in the interest rate would increase the opportunity cost of holding demand deposits only by r_d times the increase in market interest rates if competition prevented real bank earnings from increasing. This is the increased opportunity costs to banks of holding required reserves. As a result, the net change in the opportunity cost of holding demand deposits which results from a change in market interest rates may, in fact, be quite small. The interest rate effect on the demand for money would consequently be small, making the LM schedule nearly vertical.

VII. A RECAP

It is perhaps useful at this point to recapitulate briefly the elements of the determinants of nominal aggregate demand. We started with the circular flow of income and noticed that a determinant of the absolute price level at full employment and, hence, a determinant of nominal income was derived by looking at net additions to the supply of funds in the economy that can be used to finance GNP expenditures and net leakages out of the circular flow of income. The only net additions to funds available for GNP expenditures other than those generated by the sale of goods and services are increases in the money supply. The only net leakage balancing these additional sources of funds is hoarding, or increases in the demand for nominal cash balances. Finally, to determine why there might be a change in the demand for cash balances we specified a simplified liquidity preference function and noted that the ratio of desired cash balances to nominal income may be changed by alterations in the interest rate due to pure fiscal policy actions and the like.

We shall now derive a simplified model of the determinants of aggregate supply. Only when we are able to have a complete model of aggregate demand and aggregate supply can we determine or at least attempt to predict whether an increase in the rate of growth of nominal aggregate demand (for whatever reason) will manifest itself in either an increase in the rate of growth of output or as an increase in the rate of growth of prices (the right-hand side of equation 2–15). In other words, if we wish to attempt an assessment of the probable effects of monetary and fiscal policy, we must have a complete model of aggregate demand and aggregate supply because policy-makers presumably wish to be able to predict how much of any increase they cause in nominal aggregate demand will be translated into an increase in real output (which they want) or an increase in prices (which they don't want).

VIII. DETERMINANTS OF AGGREGATE SUPPLY AND THE DEMAND FOR LABOR

The liquidity preference function provides us with the various combinations of output and price levels which make the demand for money equal to the supply. The actual combination which will occur depends, of course, not only on the liquidity preference function, but also upon the output that producers desire to supply. This in turn depends on the labor market. In the short run we assume that labor is the only factor of production. As more workers are added without increasing the capital stock, each worker's marginal product is assumed to fall. The marginal product of labor decreases because the capital stock is assumed constant. The short-run profits of a price- and wage-taking producer are maximized when the wage rate equals the marginal revenue product of labor, or:

$$P \cdot MPL = W \qquad (2\text{--}21)$$

where P = price at which final output is sold

MPL = marginal physical product of labor

W = nominal or money wage rate

The aggregate supply schedule represents all the combinations of price and output which satisfy equation 2–21. It represents all the price levels and outputs which would make the nominal value of additional output generated by hiring additional labor equal to the nominal wages paid for that additional labor. Since the marginal product of labor falls as output and employment increase, the price level must rise to leave the nominal value of labor's marginal product unchanged. Thus, the aggregate supply schedule slopes upward in Figure 2–6. This supply sched-

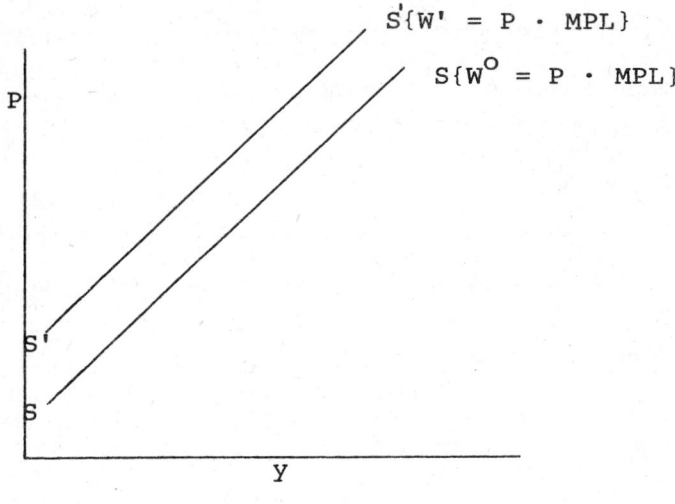

Figure 2-6

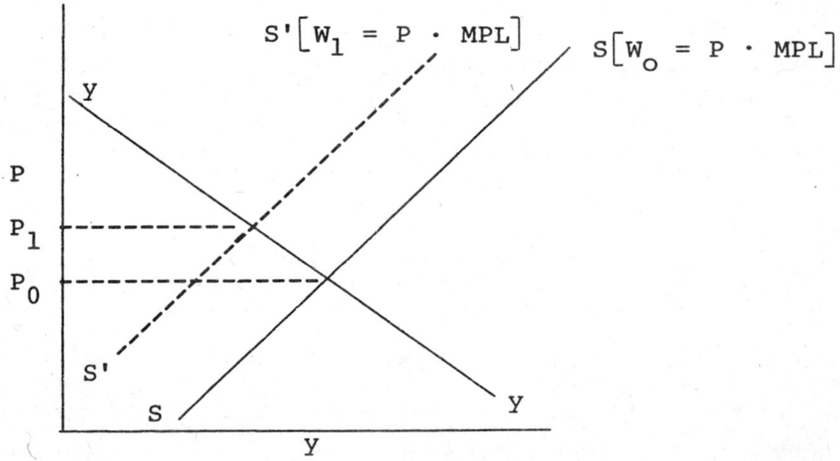

Figure 2-7

ule, SS, will shift if the wage rate changes. For example, an increase in the wage rate will shift the aggregate supply schedule SS up to S'S' in Figure 2–6 because an increase in wage rates produces a proportionate increase in prices at any level of output in this particular model.[5] For any wage rate and any money supply there will exist some combination of output and price level which simultaneously makes the demand for money equal the supply and maximizes the profits of producers. This, of course, is an equilibrium price and output combination.

A. A COBB–DOUGLAS PRODUCTION FUNCTION EXAMPLE

We will use an aggregate Cobb-Douglas production function to derive an aggregate supply schedule that can be used in analyzing actual data in the United States. (We could use a CES production function which would have a constant elasticity of substitution like the Cobb-Douglas, but that elasticity can take on any value.) In the Cobb-Douglas production function, the elasticity of factor substitution is unity and there are also constant returns to scale. Using the former characteristic we know that under conditions of competitive equilibrium the factor shares would be constant.

We shall use as our production function the following specification:

$$y = L^\alpha K^{1-\alpha} \qquad (2\text{--}22)$$

where L = labor services measured in constant quality units

K = capital services measured in constant quality units

α = elasticity of real output with respect to labor input

$1-\alpha$ = elasticity of output with respect to capital input

In a price- and wage-taker's model the equilibrium occurs whenever the nominal or money wage rate equals the price of the final product times the marginal product of labor, as represented in equation 2–21. This can be rewritten as:

$$W = P \cdot \frac{\partial y}{\partial L} \qquad (2\text{--}23)$$

---

5. If we wish to look at a noncompetitive situation, we know that short-run profits are maximized for price- and wage-makers when $P \cdot (1 \times \frac{1}{\eta})$ MPL $= W (1 + \frac{1}{\varepsilon})$, where η is the price elasticity of demand and ε is the wage elasticity of the supply of labor to the firm.

But the marginal product of labor, $\partial y/\partial L$, is equal to $\alpha(y/L)$, so that 2-23 becomes:

$$W = P \alpha \frac{y}{L} \qquad (2\text{-}24)$$

Consequently, the aggregate Cobb-Douglas production function implies that price levels and unit labor costs are proportional when producers' short-run profits are maximized.

$$P\alpha = \frac{WL}{y} = \text{unit labor cost} \qquad (2\text{-}25)$$

B. EMPIRICAL EVIDENCE

Casual empirical evidence indicates that the proportionality of prices and unit labor costs is a fairly good approximation of the secular trends in prices and unit labor costs in the United States. For example, looking at Table 2-1 we see that there is a long-run stability in the relationship between prices and unit labor costs.

Table 2-1

Period	Percentage Change per Year	
	Unit Labor Costs	Index of Prices
1947-53	3.0	3.2
1953-59	2.1	2.3
1959-66	1.1	1.3
1947-66	2.0	2.2

Source: Council of Economic Advisors, *Economic Report of the President, 1968*.

The periods used to measure the percentage change in unit labor costs and in prices were chosen so that the terminal periods would be during times of relatively high employment. Notice that there is a constant 0.2% difference in each period between the percentage rate of change in unit labor costs and the percentage rate of change in prices.

C. CYCLICAL FLUCTUATIONS

Short-run relationships, however, are not as clear-cut. There are cyclical fluctuations in the ratio of unit labor costs to prices. These fluctuations point out one of the defects of our simple aggregate supply function which assumes short-run profits are maximized. Long-run considerations cause employers to keep employees on the payroll during the recession phase of the business cycle even though their current marginal revenue product is less than their current wage rate. One explanation of this phenomenon is that the short-run costs of keeping these extra workers on the payroll are offset by the costs of rehiring or losing them to other employers if they are laid off. As a result, the ratio of prices to unit labor costs falls during recessions and rises as we approach full employment.

Moreover, labor productivity tends to be greater the closer the economy approaches full employment. The reason is that some employment within each firm is of an overhead nature. Since overhead labor is a relatively fixed factor of production, overhead labor employment varies very little with cyclical fluctuations in production. As a result output per man hour tends to increase at a rate less than the long-run average per year during the recession phase of the business cycle and greater than the long-run average per year during the recovery phase.

IX. PUTTING SUPPLY AND DEMAND TOGETHER

It is now time for us to put the elements of supply and demand together to form a simplified complete model of the economy for the purposes of analyzing changes in output and employment. We will continue to specify the liquidity preference function as in equation 2–14. We now attempt to simultaneously satisfy the aggregate demand and supply equations for output. Our supply function is given by 2–22, which, when coupled with profit maximization, yielded 2–25. Equation 2–25 may be stated as:

$$P = \frac{ULC}{\alpha} \qquad (2\text{--}26)$$

where ULC = unit labor costs

We now substitute 2–26 into the simplified liquidity preference function, 2–14, or:

$$M = kyP = ky\frac{1}{\alpha}ULC \qquad (2\text{--}27)$$

which becomes:

$$y = \frac{M}{ULC}\frac{\alpha}{k} \qquad (2\text{--}28)$$

If we want to approximate dynamic behavior in our economy, we must translate 2–28 into a moving equilibrium situation. This can be done by stating it in the following manner:

$$\triangle \ln y = \triangle \ln M - \triangle \ln k - \triangle \ln ULC \qquad (2\text{--}29)$$

Putting 2–25 into a moving equilibrium form results in:

$$\triangle \ln P = \triangle \ln ULC \qquad (2\text{--}30)$$

That is to say, the rate of change of prices will be equal to the rate of change of unit labor costs.

We have now developed a model of moving equilibrium combining both the elements of aggregate supply and aggregate demand. Changes in the rate of growth of real output in this simplified model are a function of changes in the money supply, the public's desire for nominal cash balances relative to nominal income, and changes in unit labor costs. We can use this model to distinguish two different types of inflation.

X. INFLATION: DEMAND–PULL AND COST–PUSH

Consider first the classical theory of demand-pull inflation. Demand inflation results from a situation where desired nominal expenditures on goods and services rise at a faster rate than real output at full employment. Aggregate real output is exogenously determined by the full employment of both capital and labor. The rate of change of real output at full employment is the rate of change of the labor force measured in man hours plus the rate of change of average output per man hour. In other words, we assume that there are only two sources of growth—changes in labor force and changes in average output per man hour. In any event:

$$\triangle \ln y \text{ (full employment)} = \triangle \ln N + \triangle \ln \frac{y}{N} \qquad (2\text{--}31)$$

where N = man hours of labor input (measured in constant quality units)

During the period 1955 to 1970 the basic secular rate of increase in output per man hour in the private, nonfarm sector was about 2.5% per year. Assuming that growth in productivity and an increase in man hours of about 1.75% per year, long run potential output grows at about 4.25% per year.

By rearranging the liquidity preference function 2–14 and substituting full employment real output for y, we find that:

$$P = \frac{M}{ky \text{ (full employment)}} \qquad (2\text{--}32)$$

Since we are interested in a moving equilibrium, we translate 2–32 into:

$$\triangle \ln P = \triangle \ln M - \triangle \ln k - \triangle \ln y \text{ (full employment)} \qquad (2\text{--}33)$$

And equation 2–30 still holds, of course.

$$\triangle \ln P = \triangle \ln W - \triangle \ln \frac{y}{L} = \triangle \ln ULC \qquad (2\text{--}34)$$

Hence, in the classical demand-pull model a one percent increase in the rate of increase in nominal aggregate demand would produce a one percent increase in the rate of wage increase. Wage rates are *endogenous* in this theory of inflation because output is *exogenous*, its rate of growth being determined only by changes in man hours of labor employed and changes in the average output per man hour (productivity).

An alternative theory of inflation is one in which the wage rate, rather than output, is exogenous. This is the cost-push theory of inflation. The aggregate supply schedule shifts upward independently of any increase in aggregate demand. We demonstrate this in Figure 2–7 (p. 20) where we have combined Figures 2–3 and 2–6. The shift of SS to S'S' can be caused by a spontaneous increase in wages.

If we want to translate the cost-push theory into the terms of our simultaneous solution of the aggregate demand and supply model presented above, we see that the money supply, the ratio of desired money balances to nominal income and the exogenous wage rate determine the level of real output:

$$y = \frac{M}{ULC} \frac{\alpha}{k} \qquad (2\text{--}35)$$

Given k, if the exogenous wage rate is "too high" relative to the given money supply, the equilibrium output will be less than at full employment. We are able to estimate the unemployment rate from the full employment output gap by using Okun's Law.[6] According to Okun's Law, each one percent increase in the unemployment rate is associated with a loss of three percent of real GNP:

$$U_t = U^* + \tfrac{1}{3} \left(\frac{y_t - y}{y_t}\right) 100 \qquad (2\text{–}36)$$

where U_t = the rate of unemployment in period t

y_t = full employment real income.

U^* = unemployment rate associated with full employment

XI. WEAKNESSES IN THE ABOVE TWO MODELS

Neither the classical demand-pull inflation theory nor the cost-push inflation theory are consistent with many situations which we have experienced in the United States and in other countries. The most egregious failing of the most elementary interpretation of classical demand theory of inflation is that it does not provide an explanation for fluctuations in the unemployment rate. In this model output is exogenously determined by the *full* employment of capital and labor. There can be no undesired unemployment of the factors of production.

The cost-push model, for all its intuitive appeal to observers of the economic scene, does not in the simple form presented here provide a theory of the determination of wage rates. After all, wages are presented as exogenous in this model. It is spontaneous shifts in wages which shift the supply schedule up, thus causing a rise in the price level.

In order to develop a theory of wage rate determination, we present in the following chapter an explanation of reservation wage rates. This theory coupled with elements of the models presented in this chapter will help us provide a rationale for unemployment and, further, present us with an explanation of why an inflationary recession can occur. A reconciliation of demand-pull and cost-push inflation models is thus obtained.

---

6. Arthur Okun, "Potential GNP: Its Measurement and Significance," *1962 Proceedings of the Business and Economic Statistics Section of the American Statistical Association*, pp. 98–104.

SELECTED REFERENCES

1. Brofenbrenner, Martin and F. D. Holtzman, "A Survey of Inflation Theory," *American Economic Review*, volume 53, September, 1963, pp. 593–661.
2. Friedman, Milton, "A Discussion of the Inflationary Gap," *American Economic Review*, XXXII, June, 1942, pp. 314–320.
3. Friedman, Milton, *The Optimum Quantity of Money and Other Essays*, Aldine Publishing Company (Chicago: 1969).
4. Hicks, J. R., "Mr. Keynes and the Classics," *Econometrica*, volume V, October, 1937, pp. 147–149.
5. Oi, Walter Y., "Labor as a Quasi-fixed Factor of Production," *Journal of Political Economy*, December, 1962, volume 70, pp. 538–555.
6. Smith, Warren L., "Graphical Exposition of Complete Keynesian System," *Southern Economic Journal*, volume 23, September, 1956, pp. 115–125.

CHAPTER 3. A THEORY OF INVESTMENT IN UNEMPLOYMENT

I. INTRODUCTION

We closed the last chapter by noting the related weaknesses of both the demand-pull and cost-push theories of inflation. In the former, while wages are endogenous, output is exogenously determined by the full employment of productive resources. It is impossible to use this classical theory of demand-pull inflation to explain periods of both rising prices and unemployment. In the cost-push theory, on the other hand, output is endogenous and wages are exogenous. This theory is incomplete because it contains no model which predicts inflation-causing wage changes.

In terms of the aggregate demand and supply model developed in the last section, the cost-push theory of inflation implies that unemployment is the result of wage rigidities which prevent the supply schedule from adjusting "rapidly" to nominal aggregate demand so as to produce full employment at all times. Changes in nominal aggregate demand can induce quantity rather than wage adjustments in the labor market because workers may be slow in adjusting their nominal wage demands to appropriately reflect their real wage aspirations. For example, a reduction in aggregate demand will result in unemployment if wages do not fall proportionally with prices. Figure 3–1 shows the quan-

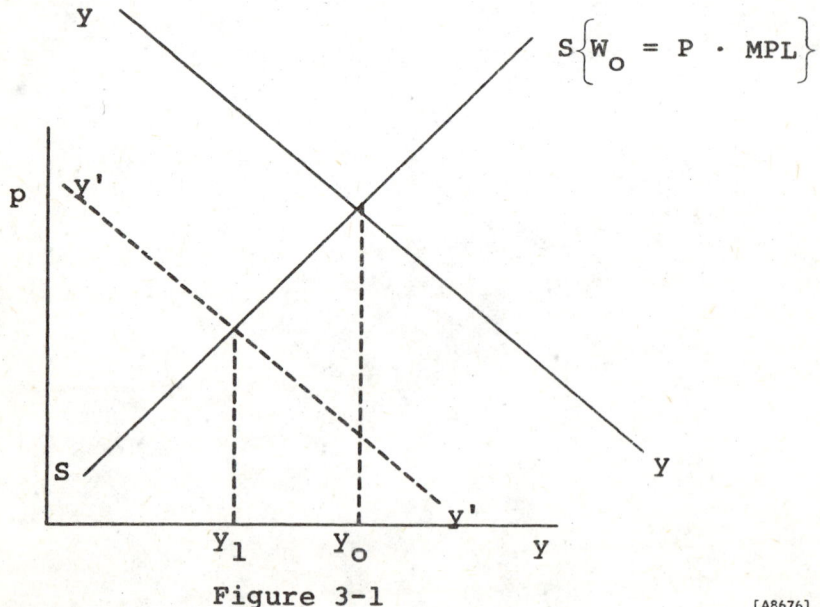

Figure 3-1

tity adjustment associated with a reduction in the aggregate demand schedule resulting from wage rigidity. The yy aggregate demand schedule shifts downward to y'y' (for whatever reason) resulting in a reduction of aggregate output from y_0 to y_1. The aggregate supply schedule SS remains fixed because of rigid wages of W_0.

In this chapter we shall consider this notion of wage rigidity in terms of a model of *search unemployment*, rather than the usual institutional constraints. In this new sense, unemployment is treated as voluntary.

II. UNEMPLOYMENT

Unemployment, whatever its cause, always receives much political attention as an indicator of hardship experienced by the working man. In reality, however, much of that unemployment consists of a worthwhile investment in the search for a better job. In a dynamic economy such as the United States', there are constant shifts in the supply and demand for workers in particular industries which necessitate changes in either relative wages or employment. Permanent shifts in relative demand away from a particular industry's product cause either cuts in wage demands or the movement of workers to other jobs in other industries. Which adjustment occurs depends on how the worker assesses his alternative employment opportunities.

Charles Holt described the facts about unemployment and the flow of workers into the unemployed category in 1969 in the following way:

> In the United States currently there are about 80 million employed workers, 3 million unemployed workers, and probably a comparable number of vacancies, but data on this are inadequate. Employment durations for all accessions average roughly 2.7 years. Unemployed workers and vacancies wait roughly a month on the average before finding work or employees. The total flow of quits and layoffs amounts to 30 million per year. Some workers even travel the quit or layoff loop several times in a year. Turnover rates of the order of 3 or 4 percent a month account for this tremendous flow. The stock of unemployed workers is replaced every month on average. Offsetting this flow from the stock of employed workers is a roughly equal flow of accessions. Employers have to recruit continually

in order to hold a constant work force. The probability that an unemployed worker will find a job is roughly 20 percent per week and gives a long-tailed exponential distribution of unemployment duration.[1]

These data indicate the part unemployment plays in the search for a new job. Much of this unemployment includes workers seeking better job opportunities of their own accord. In the process, they move from lower to higher productivity jobs, thereby contributing to economic growth.

A. SEARCH UNEMPLOYMENT

In this section we shall analyze *voluntary unemployment* as a rational choice to devote time to the search for a new job. A later section will discuss the situation where job vacancies are eliminated by minimum wage restrictions; but for the purpose of discussion here, firms are always assumed to have job vacancies. Moreover, each firm can always profit from hiring workers at a wage below their marginal revenue product.

Once a worker becomes unemployed, the duration of his unemployment depends on the costs of and the returns to obtaining *information* on alternative employment possibilities. If a worker is willing to accept a low enough wage, he can find a job almost immediately. But he usually isn't, and for very good reasons. He may be making a crucial mistake by accepting a job at a wage rate below what he could receive if he only waited. He has to wait because he does not have perfect information about the demand for his labor services. He must search for information about alternative employment opportunities. A worker, of course, does not have to become unemployed in order to search.

Obtaining information is a costly economic activity and there are various ways of engaging in this activity. If the worker decides to remain unemployed in order to do this, he is specializing in this economic endeavor. He then becomes self-employed in the task of information collection. The information he seeks concerns the array of wages and job environments which he could obtain.

---

1. Holt, Charles C., "Improving the Labor Market Tradeoff between Inflation and Unemployment," *American Economic Review*, May, 1969, p. 137.

The more one specializes, the more efficient one can become. Therefore, the unemployed worker is more efficient at obtaining information about alternative job prospects than the employed worker. However, the cost of obtaining that efficiency is wages foregone. Another cost may result from the fact that an unemployed worker is often considered to be less desirable by a new employer than an employed worker. In other words, employment itself may be a recommendation and unemployment may give an undesirable signal to prospective employers. For an already employed worker, the decision-making process merely involves a weighing of the potential marginal benefits from full-time searching with the known costs of foregoing wages.

In order to more fully develop the concept of this type of search unemployment, we will assume the following idealized situation. Under these simplifying assumptions, we can determine the appropriate *reservation wage rate* below which a rational unemployed worker rejects all wage offers and, hence, will continue to remain unemployed.

ASSUMPTIONS

1. The worker has perfect knowledge of the probability density function of relevant wage offers in the market.
2. The worker is risk-neutral; therefore, he maximizes the mathematical expectation of his wealth position.
3. Each worker receives unemployment compensation of Uc during each time period he is unemployed. (The monetary equivalent of any consumption value gained from unemployment—e. g., leisure—is included in Uc.)
4. Once a worker accepts a job, he receives that wage rate forever.

III. THE RESERVATION WAGE RATE

Let us consider a worker who has been laid off or fired from a job. He is now in a position to search out job information. Notice that we do not say he is looking for a job. He can always find a job—in fact, almost immediately—if he is willing to accept anything. The rational worker will logically formulate a reservation wage rate below which he rejects all wage offers. (Notice here that we are lumping all aspects of a job into one variable: the wage rate.) According to assumption 2 above, the reservation wage rate should be set so as to maximize the expected wealth position of the worker. For this to be true, the reservation wage rate must have the following property:

> The expected wealth position to be gained by remaining unemployed as long as wage offers are below this reservation wage rate is equal to the present value of accepting the reservation wage rate.

We can develop the salient aspects of this model by using some simple present value formulations. First, consider the present value of receiving the reservation wage rate, W_o, which is:

$$\sum_{t=0}^{\infty} \frac{W_o}{(1+r)^t} = \frac{W_o(1+r)}{r} \qquad (3\text{-}1)$$

The above equation, of course, does not tell us what W_o is. We need to be able to equate 3–1 with the expected wealth position of the worker who remains unemployed because he has not yet been offered his reservation wage. Once we do that, we can solve for W_o.

We assume that the worker is sampling wage offers from a large population of potential job prospects. In each period of unemployment, the worker receives unemployment compensation, Uc, and also samples the population for a wage offer above his reservation wage. Hence, the expected net worth of remaining unemployed until receiving a wage offer of the reservation wage rate, W_o, or better is:

$$\text{Uc} + \sum_{t=1}^{\infty} \frac{H(\hat{W})}{(1+r)^t} \qquad (3\text{-}2)$$

$$+ (1-\pi)\left(\frac{\text{Uc}}{1+r}\right) + (1-\pi)\sum_{t=2}^{\infty} \frac{H(\hat{W})}{(1+r)^t}$$

$$+ (1-\pi)^2 + \frac{\text{Uc}}{(1+r)^2}) + (1-\pi)^2 \sum_{t=3}^{\infty} \frac{H(\hat{W})}{(1+r)^t}$$

$$+ (1-\pi)^3 \left(\frac{\text{Uc}}{(1+r)^3}\right)$$

$$+ (1-\pi)^3 \sum_{t=4}^{\infty} \frac{H(\hat{W})}{(1+r)^t} + \cdots$$

where r = rate of discount

π = probability of accepting a job offer in any one period

($\pi = \int_{W_o}^{\infty} f(\hat{W})\, d\hat{W}$ where $f(\hat{W})$ is the probability density function of wage offers)

$$H(\hat{W}) = \int_{W_o}^{\infty} \hat{W} f(\hat{W})\, d\hat{W}$$

The probability of accepting a wage offer, π, is equal to:

$$\int_{W_o}^{\infty} f(\hat{W})\, d\hat{W} \qquad (3\text{-}3)$$

where $f(\hat{W})$ is the probability density function of wage offers

With the distribution of wage offers known, we can compute the probability of a wage offer of W_o or greater occurring, as can be seen in Figure 3–2.

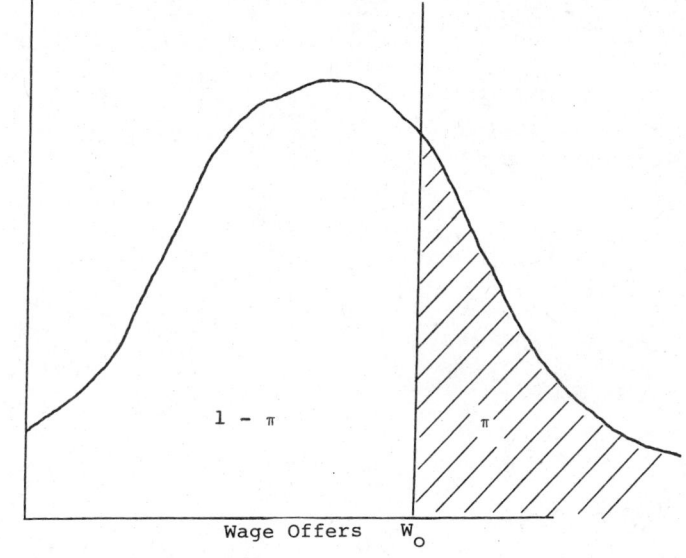

Figure 3-2

Probability of Accepting a Job Offer

A. FINDING THE RESERVATION WAGE

Fortunately, equation 3-2 can be simplified. It becomes:

$$\frac{Uc\,(1+r)}{r+\pi} + \frac{H(W)'\,(1+r)}{r(r+\pi)} \tag{3-4}$$

Thus, the optimal wage rate has the following property:

$$\frac{W_o\,(1+r)}{r} = \frac{Uc\,(1+r)}{r+\pi} + \frac{H(\hat{W})'\,(1+r)}{r(r+\pi)} \tag{3-5}$$

If we multiply 3-5 by $r/(1+r)'$, we obtain an expression for the optimal reservation wage rate:

$$W_o = \frac{rUc + H(\hat{W})}{r+\pi} \tag{3-6}$$

The optimal reservation wage rate will be higher the higher unemployment compensation and the higher the mean of the probability density function of wage offers, holding the form of the probability density function constant. Moreover, unemployment in this model has the nature of investment, making it negatively related to the real rate of discount. Voluntary employment represents a deliberate choice of lower current income in exchange for a higher expected value of future income. As a result, the average *duration* of unemployment should be negatively related to the rate of discount. From equation 3-6 we can see that an increase in the rate of discount, r, will reduce the optimal reservation wage and increase the probability of acceptance, π, since:

$$\frac{d\left(\frac{rUc + H(\hat{W})}{r+\pi}\right)}{dr} = \frac{\pi Uc - H(\hat{W})}{(r+\pi)^2} < 0$$

so long as

$$Uc < \frac{H(\hat{W})}{\pi}$$

IV. THE DURATION OF UNEMPLOYMENT

The number of unemployed workers in the economy is equal to the flow of workers into the unemployed category from quits, layoffs, and new entrants into the labor force times the average duration of unemployment. We see in Figure 3-3 that since the mid-1950s, the average duration of unemployment has ranged from a high of over 16 weeks in 1961 to a low of less than 8 weeks in 1969. The average duration of unemployment started a steady rise with the onset of the 1969–70 recession, as can clearly be seen in Figure 3–3. The series on duration of unemployment is approximately coincident with the series on the level of unemployment, as seen in Figure 3–4.

Figure 3–3

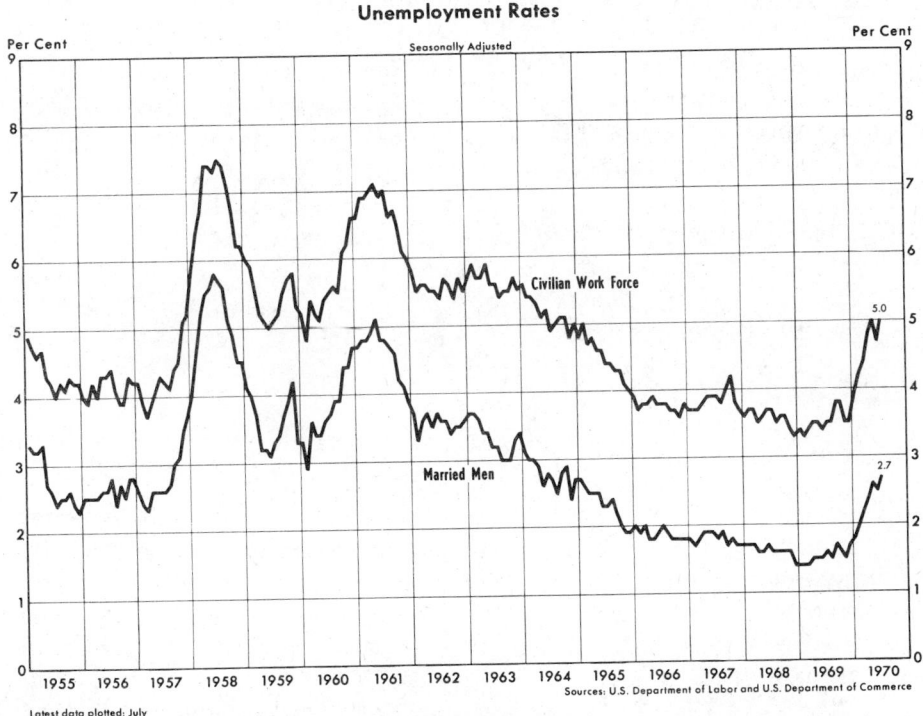

Figure 3–4

The duration of unemployment, T, is a random variable with a geometric distribution which takes on the following form:

$$\text{Prob}(T = t) = \pi(1-\pi)^{t-1} \qquad (3\text{-}7)$$

We can find the expected duration of unemployment by:

$$\sum_{t=1}^{\infty} t\pi(1-\pi)^{t-1} = \frac{1}{\pi} = E(T) \qquad (3\text{-}8)$$

In other words, the expected duration of unemployment, E(T), is equal to the reciprocal of the probability of accepting a job offer in any one period, this probability being obtained from setting the optimal reservation wage rate, 3–6, and then computing the shaded area, π, in Figure 3–2. If the probability of accepting a job offer in any one period is 1, then the expected duration of unemployment is 1 also. That is, the worker accepts a job in the period in which he becomes unemployed. In other words, the period of unemployment is trivial. (This situation may characterize planned economies such as in the Soviet Union and China.) As the probability of accepting a wage offer above the reservation wage rate falls, of course, the expected duration of unemployment increases.

Now consider the flow of workers into the unemployed category from quits, layoffs, firings, and new entrants into the labor force. We will define F_t as the flow of workers into the unemployed category during time period t. The number of workers unemployed at time period t, U_t, will be equal to the flow of workers into the unemployed category during the current time period plus the flow of workers in previous time periods who still have not received a wage offer above their reservation wage rate.

$$U_t = \sum_{x=0}^{\infty} F_{t-x}(1-\pi)^x \qquad (3\text{-}9)$$

Remember that the quantity $(1-\pi)$ is equal to the probability of *not* accepting a wage offer at or above the reservation wage rate. It is equal to the unshaded area in Figure 3–2.

If the flow of workers into the unemployed category is constant—that is, $F_t = F_o$ for all t—then we can simplify equation

3–9 by multiplying F_o times the expected duration of unemployment obtained from 3–8, or:

$$U_t = \sum_{x=0}^{\infty} F_o (1-\pi)^{t-x} = \frac{F_o}{\pi} = F_o\, E(T) \qquad (3\text{–}10)$$

In this situation, the number of unemployed workers is equal to the constant flow of workers into the stock of unemployed times the expected duration of unemployment. Whenever the expected duration of unemployment rises, so, too, will the unemployment rate even though the flow into the unemployment category has not changed. During changes in the business cycle, this often occurs. Politicians become alarmed at a significant jump in U_t even though it may only mean, with a constant F_t, that the duration of unemployment has increased by a week or two.

A. WHERE THE VARIANCE OF THE PROBABILITY DENSITY FUNCTION IS ZERO

So far we have only discussed the mean of the probability density function of wage offers. However, another important parameter to consider is the dispersion or variance of this density function. The reservation wage rate and π depend critically on the variance. To understand this, let us take an extreme case first. In the extreme situation where the variance of this function is zero, the marginal revenue product of labor is the same in all firms; hence, the mean of the density function of *all* wage offers, $\bar{W}$, is identical to every wage offer. There are no inter-industry differences in marginal revenue product. Of course, no one will search for jobs in this situation. This is similar to having perfect information about all job offers. Here in fact each worker does have perfect information; every job offers the same wage rate. No one will find it profitable to remain unemployed and search for additional prospects unless, of course, unemployment compensation, Uc, is greater than or equal to the wage rate, $\bar{W}$. In that situation workers would remain unemployed indefinitely because:

$$\bar{W} < \frac{rUc + \bar{W}}{r + \pi} \qquad (3\text{–}11)$$

when $\pi = 1$ and $Uc > \bar{W}$.[2]

---

2. Note that $\bar{W}$ is defined as the mean of the entire frequency distribution of wage offers, whereas $H(\hat{W})/\pi$ is the mean of the distribution of wage offers that are equal to or greater than the optimal reservation rate, W_0.

B. VARIANCE OF PROBABILITY DENSITY FUNCTION IS GREATER THAN ZERO

Consider the example in which we hold π constant but increase the variance of the probability density function of wage offers. The only thing that changes in this situation is the reservation wage. We have two possibilities:

1. If the initial optimum reservation wage, W_o, is less than the mean, $\bar{W}$, the new reservation wage (not necessarily optimal) associated with a constant π (greater than 0.5) will have to fall. This can be most easily seen by considering Figure 3-5. We start with a probability density function of

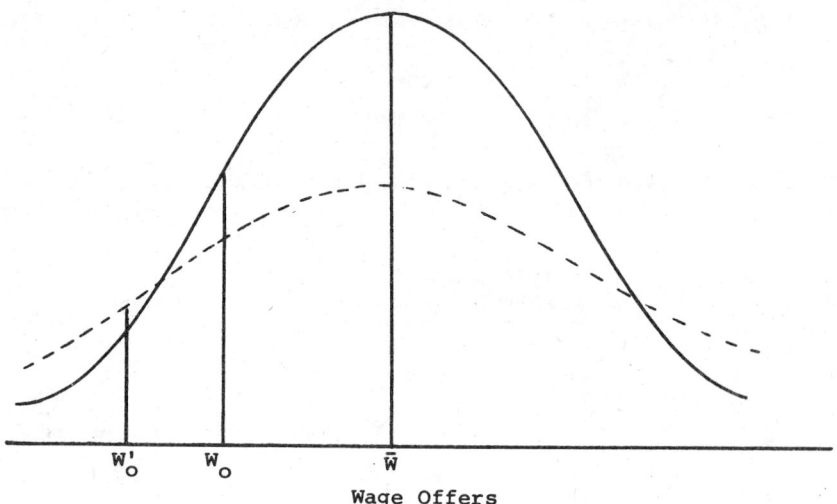

Figure 3-5

wage offers represented by the solid line. The mean of that density function is $\bar{W}$. By assumption the initial reservation wage is $W_o < \bar{W}$. Now we increase the variance of this density function. The reservation wage associated with a constant π must move to the left from W_o to W'_o. At the same time, $H(\hat{W})/\pi$—the mean of the distribution of wage offers that are equal to or greater than the optimal reservation rate—must increase.

Now consider the initial optimal reservation wage defined by:

$$W_o = \frac{rUc + H(\hat{W})}{r + \pi} \tag{3-6'}$$

If we divide through by π, 3-6 becomes:

$$W_o = \frac{\frac{r}{\pi}Uc + \frac{H(\hat{W})}{\pi}}{\frac{r}{\pi} + 1} \tag{3-6'}$$

Since the increase in variance holding π constant causes W_o to fall, and $H(\hat{W})/\pi$ to rise, the right-hand side of 3-6' exceeds W'_o. Hence, the optimal reservation wage must be greater than W'_o in Figure 3-5, thereby reducing π.

2. Now consider the case where the initial optimal reservation wage, W_o, is greater than $\bar{W}$, as in Figure 3-6. The increase

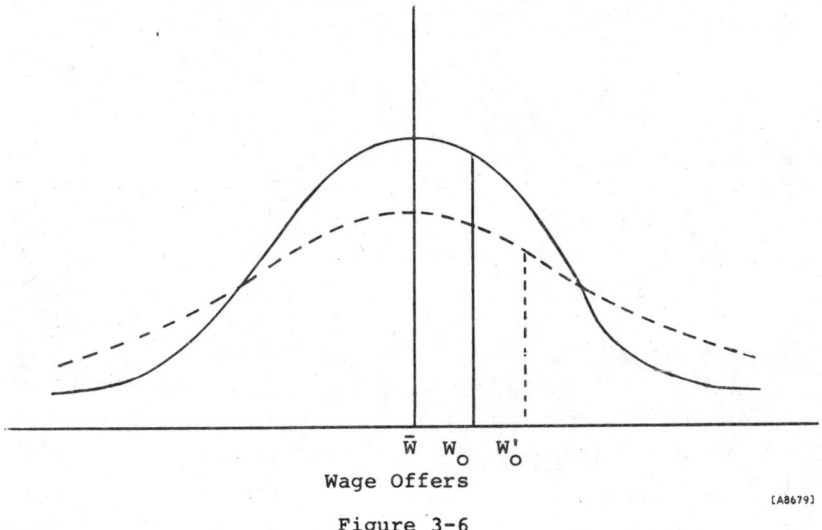

Wage Offers

Figure 3-6

in the variance of the probability density function of wage offers will shift the reservation wage associated with a constant π to the right as represented by the distance $W'_o - W_o$. Moreover, if new wage offers (W') are formed by a linear change in scale, holding the mean constant, i. e., $W' = \bar{W} + \alpha (W - \bar{W})$ where $\alpha > 1$,

$$\frac{(W'_0 - \bar{W})}{(W_0 - \bar{W})} = \frac{\left(\frac{H(\hat{W}')}{\pi} - \bar{W}\right)}{\left(\frac{H(\hat{W})}{\pi} - \bar{W}\right)}$$

Consequently, the reservation wage associated with a constant π will increase, but by less than the right-hand side of equation 3–6',

$$W'_0 < \frac{\frac{r}{\pi} Uc + \frac{H(\hat{W})}{\pi}}{\frac{r}{\pi} + 1}$$

so long as

$$(W_0 - \bar{W}) < \frac{\frac{H(\hat{W})}{\pi} - \bar{W}}{1 + \frac{r}{\pi}}$$

In either case, individuals will no longer accept the initial optimal reservation wage rate associated with a constant π. The optimum π must necessarily fall, increasing the average duration of unemployment. Consequently, the greater the variance in the marginal revenue product of labor in different sectors of the economy, the longer will be the optimal average duration of unemployment. In other words, the more interindustry differences there are in wage rates, *ceteris paribus*, the longer the expected duration of unemployment. If workers' marginal revenue product were essentially the same in all industries, the average duration of unemployment would be very small, indeed.

V. SEARCH UNEMPLOYMENT AND ERRORS IN FORECASTING

In the above we have assumed that unemployed individuals know the probability density function of relevant wage offers. That is, both the variance and the mean, $\bar{W}$, are known. However, workers can make mistakes in their forecasting of the actual relative frequency distribution and, hence, these forecast errors serve as a rationalization of fluctuations in search unemployment.

Let us take an example where the individual worker has full knowledge of the relevant real wage offer distribution, but he does not know the nominal wage rates corresponding to appropriate real wages. If he predicts correctly, he will clearly invest the optimum amount of time in search unemployment. However, if his estimate of the nominal wage rate is too high, he will set his reservation wage rate too high, and he will invest too much time in search unemployment. That is to say, the average duration of unemployment will be too long; π will be too low. On the other hand, when his estimate of the nominal wage rate is too low, he will set his reservation wage rate below the optimal level and therefore invest a suboptimum amount of time in search unemployment. That is, the average duration of unemployment will be too short.

For the economy as a whole, then, any unanticipated increase in the rate of inflation and, hence, wage offers, will produce a reduction in the average duration of unemployment. However, we should not immediately jump to the conclusion that this reduction in the average duration of unemployment (and so, too, in the unemployment rate if F_t remains constant) implies an improvement in economic welfare. In the long run, labor can only increase its real wages by increasing its marginal productivity. One important source of advances in productivity is the redistribution of labor from sectors of the economy where labor's marginal productivity is low to sectors where it is high. In situations where the actual mean of wage offers exceeds its expected value—i. e., periods of unanticipated inflation—workers will underinvest in their search for job offers. The additional employment and the production created when workers accept jobs too soon are worth less than the job seeking time displaced. Whenever an unanticipated inflation or an unanticipated acceleration in the rate of inflation reduces the average duration of unemployment, *ceteris paribus*, the rate of labor's productivity growth will be reduced because workers will reduce their investment in the search for the highest paying job. They will not optimally search for job offers in which their marginal revenue product is highest.

A. SPECIFICATION OF THE RELATIONSHIP

We have just established that forecasting errors in estimating the mean of the distribution of nominal wage offers can cause fluctuations in the average duration of unemployment. Whenever the expected mean of nominal wage offers is greater than the actual mean, workers will set their reservation wage rates too high, and the average duration of unemployment will be too long. Alternatively, whenever the expected mean of job offers is less than the actual mean, the converse will be true. A linear approximation of this relationship is:

$$100 (\ln W^* - \ln \bar{W}) = \lambda (Ur - Ur^*) \qquad (3\text{--}12)$$

where W^* = forecast nominal wage mean

$\bar{W}$ = actual nominal wage mean

Ur = actual unemployment rate

Ur^* = optimal unemployment rate

The optimal unemployment rate, Ur^*, is found by obtaining the optimal π from the optimal reservation wage rate based on a correct forecast of $\bar{W}$. From equation 3–10 we can see that the optimal rate of unemployment is equal to the flow of workers into the stock of unemployed as a proportion of the total labor force times the optimal average duration of unemployment.[3]

Let's assume now that in all past periods unemployed workers had perfect knowledge of the distribution of nominal wage offers. However, the unemployed worker today is ignorant of current market data. In other words, only the past is known; the present and the future are unknown. Now, since each wage offer represents the marginal revenue product of labor in that firm, the worker's forecast of the current wage mean is formulated by extrapolating the known historical nominal wage mean into the present. This is done by looking at the latest period's nominal wage rate and adding the expected rate of inflation and the expected rate of increase in labor's marginal product. In this

---

3. A rise in the average duration of unemployment may in fact induce a partially offsetting reduction in F_t, the flow of workers into the stock of unemployed. Presumably, though, the net effect of a rise in the average duration of unemployment will be an increase in the unemployment rate.

manner, the worker obtains a forecast of the nominal marginal revenue product of labor. Hence, for a price- and wage-taker:

$$\ln W^* = \ln \bar{W}^\circ + \triangle \ln P^* + \triangle \ln \left(\frac{dy}{dL}\right)^* \qquad (3\text{-}13)$$

where W^* = forecast wage mean

$\bar{W}^\circ$ = actual wage mean in the previous time period

$\triangle \ln P^*$ = expected rate of inflation

$\triangle \ln \left(\frac{dy}{dL}\right)^*$ = expected rate of increase in labor's marginal productivity

The actual wage mean, $\bar{W}$, is, of course:

$$\ln \bar{W} = \ln \bar{W}^\circ + \triangle \ln P + \triangle \ln \left(\frac{dy}{dL}\right) \qquad (3\text{-}14)$$

where $\bar{W}$ = actual wage mean

$\triangle \ln P$ = actual rate of inflation

$\triangle \ln \left(\frac{dy}{dL}\right)$ = actual rate of increase in labor's marginal productivity

We assume that workers can anticipate their rate of increase in marginal productivity accurately; that is, the worker knows the distribution of real wage offers. The only variable left to forecast, then, is the expected rate of inflation. This allows us to obtain the following specification of the relationship between the rate of unemployment and the forecast error in estimating the rate of inflation. We need to subtract 3–14 from 3–13 and substitute the result into 3–12. Since the expected and the actual rate of increase of labor's marginal product are equal, the difference between the forecast wage mean and the actual wage mean becomes the difference between the forecasted rate of inflation and the actual rate of inflation. Therefore, 3–12 becomes:

$$100 \left(\triangle \ln P^* - \triangle \ln P\right) = \lambda \left(Ur - Ur^*\right) \qquad (3\text{-}15)$$

In other words, the difference between the actual unemployment rate, Ur, and the optimal unemployment rate, Ur*, is positively related to the difference between the predicted and the actual rate of inflation. In this form the search unemployment model has the characteristic structure of an empirical "accelerationist" Phillips curve. The greater the difference between the rate of inflation and the expected rate of inflation, the smaller the unemployment rate, and vice versa. With stable expectations of inflation, the rate of inflation would be negatively related to the unemployment rate. In periods like 1969–70, however, the rate of inflation was, in fact, positively related to the unemployment rate. In 1969, 3.5% of the labor force was without jobs. Prices increased at an annual rate of slightly less than 5%. By 1970, however, the unemployment rate had risen to 5.5% and prices were rising at almost 6%. By using 3–15, we can see that the *positive* relationship during this period between the rate of inflation and unemployment indicated that the *expected* rate of inflation was accelerating faster than the *actual* rate.

B. THE FRIEDMAN THEORY OF THE PHILLIPS CURVE RELATIONSHIP

In addition to the "search model" of unemployment developed in this chapter, there are other interpretations of the Phillips curve relationship which emphasize the importance of price expectations. The Friedman interpretation [4] is based on the assumption that employers adjust to an unanticipated inflation more rapidly than do employees. As a result there is a simultaneous fall in ex post real wages to employers and a rise in ex ante real wages to employees. Employers will have an incentive to hire more workers. Workers will simultaneously desire to increase their current supply of labor services because current ex ante real wages are high relative to their long-run expected values. This interpretation of intertemporal substitution of work effort contributes to our understanding of fluctuations in the aggregate labor supply conditions during unanticipated inflation.

C. INSTITUTIONAL CONSIDERATIONS

Much of the literature on the Phillips curve has noted that market imperfections aggravate unemployment. In many sectors of the labor market, job vacancies are eliminated by minimum wage restrictions. For instance, collective bargaining usually limits vacancies by setting floors on wage offers. Under the collective bargaining provisions of the Wagner Act, elections certify a union to negotiate wage contracts for all employees in the bargaining unit. Where collective bargaining agreements

---

4. Friedman, Milton, "The Role of Monetary Policy," *American Economic Review* (March, 1968), pp. 1–17.

succeed in raising wage rates above the competitive level, there will be an excess supply of labor to that sector of the economy. Some workers may be involuntarily laid off even though they would be willing to work at wage rates below the union's floor rather than lose their jobs. Quit rates would be low because employees realize employment opportunities elsewhere will not be as attractive. Long lists of applicants for scarce vacancies characterize those union sectors where relative wage advantages have been obtained through collective bargaining.

Some employers limit job vacancies even in the absence of unions. The costs of hiring and training new employees represents a considerable sunk investment by the employer which can be lost if the employee quits his job. If "tenured" and newly hired workers must receive roughly the same wage rate, employers have an incentive to pay wages above the market clearing level to reduce labor turnover. The result is the rationing of jobs by employers at a wage which creates excess supply of labor.

We shall discuss these market imperfections in greater detail in Chapter 6. For the present we emphasize that wage floors which contribute to unemployment are also susceptible to manipulation by unanticipated changes in aggregate demand. Typically, union wage differentials have fallen during periods of unanticipated inflation, reducing layoffs and increasing job vacancies.

In the following chapter we examine the possibilities of using the Phillips curve tradeoff as a policy tool.

SELECTED REFERENCES

1. Alchian, A.A., "Information Costs, Pricing, and Resource Unemployment," *Western Economic Journal*, volume 7, June, 1969, pp. 107–128.
2. Gordon, Donald F. and John Allan Hynes, "On the Theory of Price Dynamics," in *Microeconomic Foundation of Employment and Inflation Theory*, Phelps, E.S., et al., W.W. Norton, New York, 1970, pp. 369–393.
3. Holt, C.C., "How Can the Phillips Curve be Moved to Reduce both Inflation and Unemployment?" *American Economic Review*, May, 1969.

CHAPTER 4. THE TRADE–OFF BETWEEN UNEMPLOYMENT AND INFLATION

A monetary economy, we shall find, is essentially one in which changing views about the future are capable of influencing the quantity of employment and not merely its direction.[1]

I. INTRODUCTION

The relationship between unemployment and inflation was empirically documented by A. W. Phillips [2] and consequently is known as the Phillips curve. Phillips looked at data for the United Kingdom for the years 1861 to 1957. He tested the hypothesis that the percentage rate of change of nominal wage rates can be explained by the percentage rate of unemployment and also by the rate of change of this unemployment rate. It is interesting to note that Phillips concluded that the relationship was quite stable over the whole period studied, in spite of the changing institutional characteristics of the wage-determining process. According to Phillips' analysis, fundamental economic variables affecting wage rates remained the same throughout this period, at least at the United Kingdom.

Of course, Phillips did not postulate a strictly linear relationship as we did in the last chapter. In fact, he made a point of the highly nonlinear nature of his Phillips curve:

> When the demand for labor is high and there are very few unemployed, we should expect employers to bid wage rates up quite rapidly, each firm in each industry being continually tempted to offer a little above the prevailing rates to attract the most suitable labor from other firms and industries. On the other hand, it appears that workers are reluctant to offer their services at less than the prevailing rates when the demand for

---

1. Keynes, J. M., *The General Theory of Employment, Interest and Money*, p. vii.

2. Phillips, A. W., "The Relationship between Unemployment and the Rate of Change of Money Wage Rates in the United Kingdom, 1861–1957," *Economica*, volume 25, November, 1958, pp. 283–299.

labor is low and unemployment is high, so that wage rates fall only very slowly. The relationship between unemployment and the rate of change of wage rates is therefore likely to be highly non-linear.[3]

In order to put his theory into an empirical relationship, he chose the following form:

$$\frac{1}{W} \frac{dW}{dt} = a + bU^{-1} \qquad (4\text{--}1)$$

where W = nominal wage rates

t = time

U = unemployment rate

Phillips' empirical conclusions supported his general hypothesis and he indicated that with productivity increases of 2% per year the price level would remain relatively stable if the unemployment rate remained at 2½%.[4]

Following Phillips' work, studies on the American economy began to appear, one of the first being Bowen's study of *Wage Behavior in the Post World War Period—An Empirical Analysis*.[5] His results indicated that unemployment and nominal wage changes were related in the same manner that Phillips postulated. For example, he found that the average rate of change in the nominal wage rate in recession periods (when unemployment is relatively high) was only 3.9%, but in prosperity periods it was 6.3%. The same year a key article by Samuelson and Solow appeared in the *Proceedings of the American Economic Association*.[6] In that article Samuelson and Solow presented their views on the trade-off between inflation and unemployment:

1. In order to have wages increase at no more than the 2½ percent per annum characteristic of our productivity growth, the American economy would seem on the basis of twentieth century and post war experience to have to undergo something like 5 to 6 percent of the civilian labor force's being unemployed. That much unemployment

---

3. *Ibid.*, p. 283.

4. *Ibid.*, p. 299. Note also that to make British unemployment figures comparable to those in the United States, they should be increased about 50%.

5. William G. Bowen, Princeton, New Jersey, Princeton University Press, 1960.

6. Paul Anthony Samuelson and Robert M. Solow, "Analytical Aspects of Anti-Inflation Policy," *American Economic Review*, May, 1960.

would appear to be the cost of price stability in the years immediately ahead.

2. In order to achieve the nonperfectionist's goal of high enough output to give us no more than 3 percent unemployment, the price index might have to rise by as much as 4 to 5 percent per year. That much price rise would seem to be the necessary cost of high employment and production in the years immediately ahead.[7]

The Phillips curve relationship between changes in employment and changes in the price level appears to offer a choice between higher rates of inflation and less unemployment, or lower rates of inflation and more unemployment. The policy-makers' dilemma in this situation may be represented by Figure 4-1.

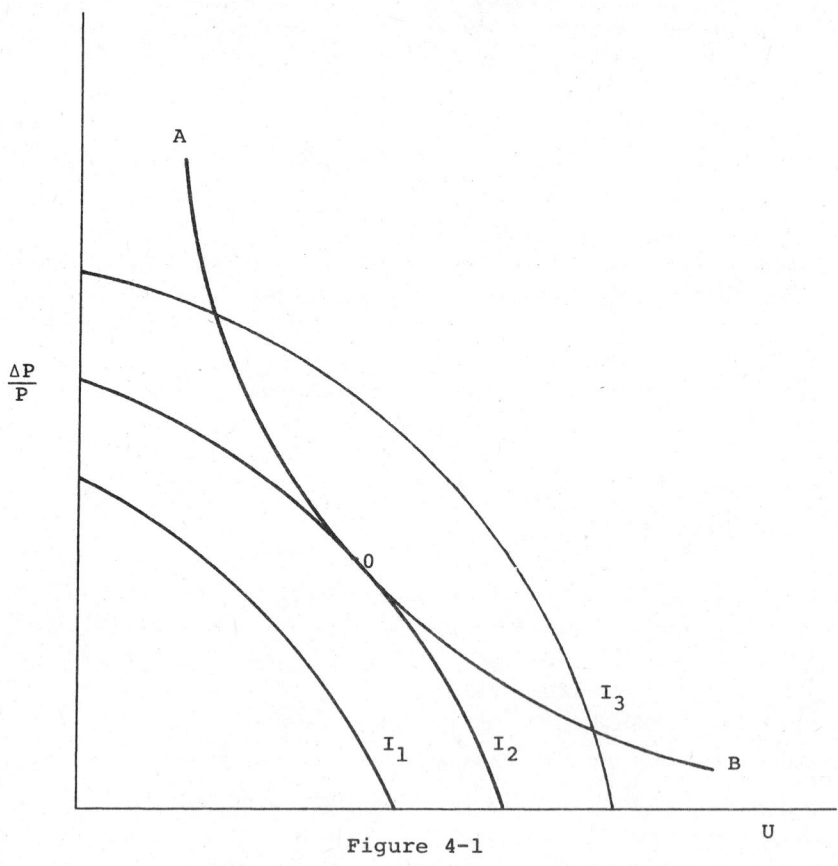

Figure 4-1

The Policy-Makers' Dilemma

7. *Ibid.*, p. 192.

On the horizontal axis is the rate of unemployment. On the vertical axis is the rate of inflation. The curve AB depicts the Phillips curve trade-off. Since both unemployment and inflation are economic "bads," the indifference curves I_1, I_2, I_3, depict decreasing levels of collective utility. The highest attainable level of utility would occur at tangency point 0.

While the analysis so far seems almost trivial, even if all the assumptions underlying it were correct, policy-makers' choices would not be that easy. If the deleterious effects of inflation were felt by one social or economic class and the effects of unemployment by another, then the trade-off would involve quite a bit more than first meets the eye. The redistribution of income would make it difficult to derive a measure of collective utility. We know, for example, that an *unanticipated* inflation hurts those who hold fixed money income-bearing assets (creditors) and helps those who issued the assets in the first place (debtors).[8]

A study by Rees and Hamilton,[9] however, indicated no statistically significant relationship between the "normal" rate of unemployment and the rate of increase of nominal wages. They concluded, ". . . we regard the construction of a plausible Phillips curve from annual data for a long period of time as a *tour de force* somewhat comparable to writing the Lord's Prayer on the head of a pin, rather than as a guide to policy." They concluded, ". . . the authors of Phillips curves would do well to label them conspicuously 'unstable—apply with extreme care.' "

More recently, papers by Friedman, Phelps, Gordon and Hynes, and others have indicated that Phillips curves depend critically upon expectations of wage and price change. If expectations of inflation depend upon past rates of inflation, the attempts to operate on today's Phillips curve can change tomorrow's trade-offs.

---

8. Note, however, that the Phillips Curve was originally interpreted as suggesting a relationship between *equilibrium* values, hence the "cost" is the welfare cost of inflation.

9. A. R. Rees and M. T. Hamilton, "The Wage-Price-Productivity Perplex," *Journal of Political Economy*, volume 75, February 1967, pp. 63–70.

II. THE UNITED STATES' EMPIRICAL RELATIONSHIP

Before we discuss the "accelerationist" analysis of the Phillips curve relationship, it is instructive to look at recent U. S. experience. Figure 4–2 shows the relationship between the rate

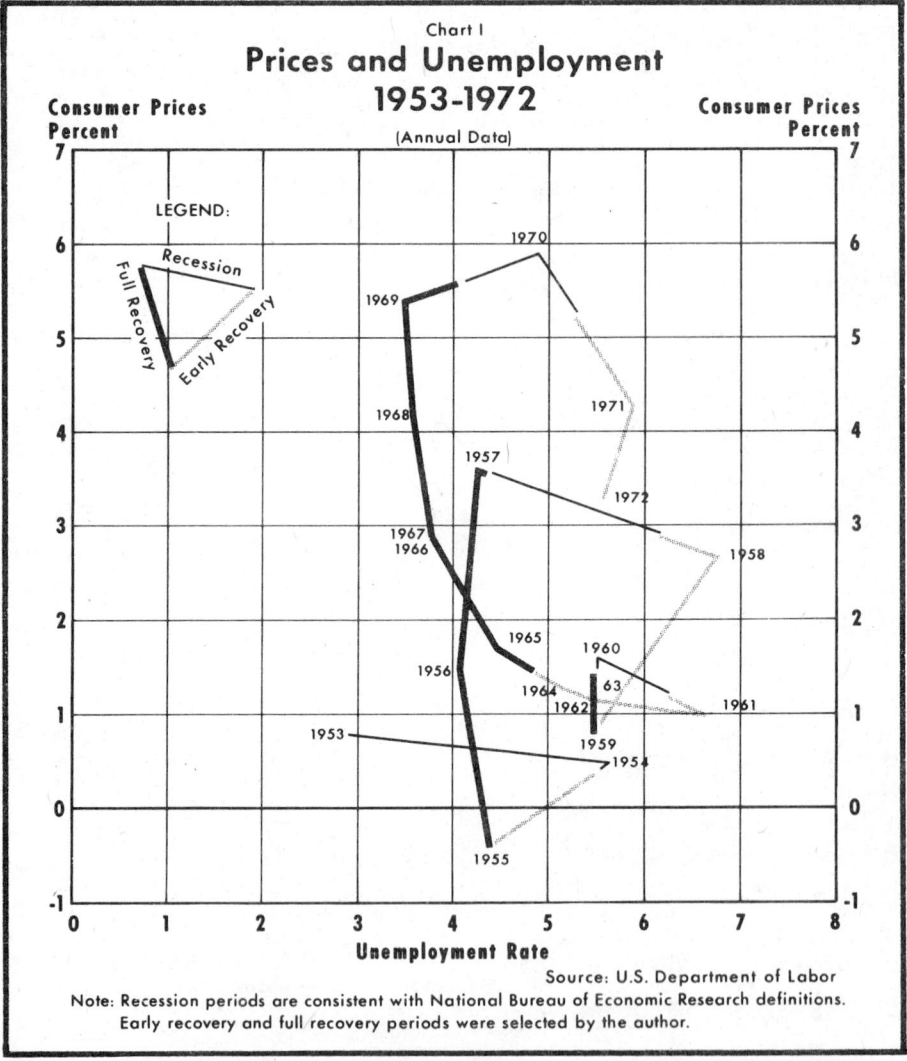

Figure 4–2

of change of consumer prices and unemployment. We show the period from post-Korean War until 1972. Roger Spencer has noted that there are apparently three distinct phases of the relationship between rates of inflation and the unemployment rate.[10] In the early recovery period of the business cycle the rate of inflation and the unemployment rate both tend to fall. This tendency results from a downward revision of inflationary expectations and cyclical productivity increases. (During the recovery phase of the business cycle output per man hour rises more rapidly and those productivity increases reduce the rate of inflation associated with a given increase in nominal wage rates.) Once the unemployment rate falls to the neighborhood of about 4.5%, though, an accelerating rate of inflation is necessary to produce further reductions in the unemployment rate. When the growth of aggregate demand is finally slowed in order to reduce inflationary pressures, the unemployment rate increases with only minor reductions in the rate of inflation.

In fact, during the 1969-70 recession phase inflation and the unemployment rate increased simultaneously. Presumably this was due to a delayed upward revision of the expected rate of inflation, reflecting the accelerating inflation of the recent past. Cyclical declines in output per man hour during the recession phase of the business cycle also contribute to price increases.

Otto Eckstein and Roger Brinner [11] have further specified the empirical relationship for the period 1955 through 1970. They explain the expected rate of price change effect on the Phillips curve relationship in terms of an "inflation severity factor." Whether or not there is a permanent trade-off between inflation and unemployment depends critically upon whether individuals correctly anticipate the rate of inflation. If an increase in the rate of inflation is never fully anticipated, a trade-off between inflation and unemployment exists. High rates of inflation can permanently lower the rate of unemployment. On the other hand, if higher rates of inflation are eventually fully anticipated, they cannot permanently lower the unemployment rate. Eckstein and Brinner empirically concluded:

> Our basic wage equation contains a non-linear form for the price variable. So long as the rate of inflation remains below 2.5 percent a year, as measured by the deflator for

10. Roger Spencer, "The National Plans to Curb Unemployment and Inflation," *Federal Reserve Bank of St. Louis Review*, Vol. 55, April, 1973.

11. Eckstein and Brinner, "The Inflation Process in the United States," Joint Economic Committee, Congress of the U.S., February 22, 1972.

consumer expenditures, the coefficient on prices is .496, with a mean lag of one-quarter and a distribution of the lag stretching back only three periods. However, when the rate of price inflation exceeds 2.5 percent, the price coefficient rises gradually to unity.[12]

In other words, for every one percentage point increase in the rate of inflation below 2.5%, the expected rate of inflation increases by only one-half percentage point. Consequently, the gap between the actual and expected rates of inflation widen, permanently reducing the unemployment rate. However, for rates of inflation greater than 2.5%, an increase in the rate of inflation cannot permanently lower the unemployment rate because the expected rate of inflation will eventually rise by a similar amount preventing the difference between the actual and expected rates of inflation from increasing. Obviously, there is an implication that in the short run, until expectations have fully adjusted, a trade-off exists.

We can illustrate the hypothesized permanent trade-off between unemployment and inflation when rates of inflation are below 2½% per annum in Figure 4-3. The actual rate of infla-

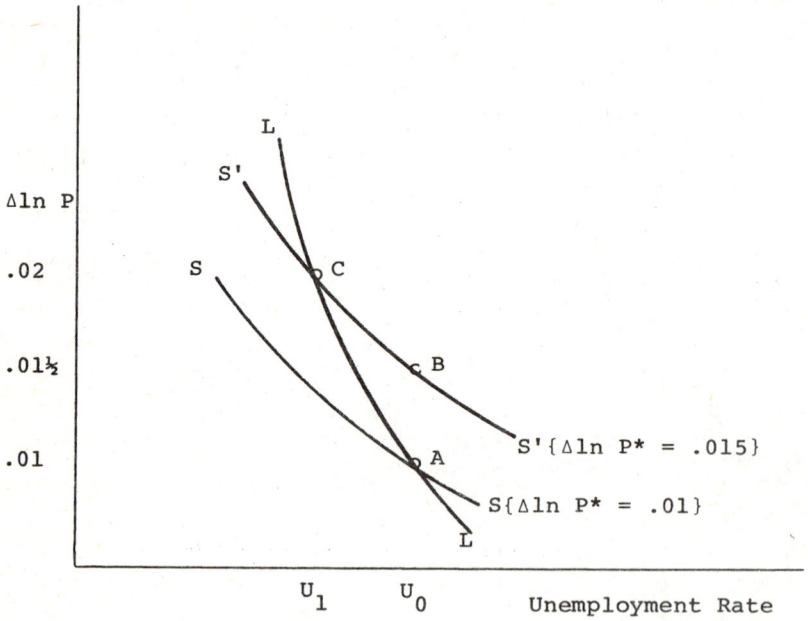

Figure 4-3

12. *Ibid.*, p. 13.

tion, $\triangle \ln P$, is measured on the vertical axis, the unemployment rate on the horizontal axis. SS measures the short-run trade-off when the expected rate of inflation is 1% per year. We start out at point A with 1% of unemployment. Now, assume that the rate of inflation increases to 2%. The implication of Eckstein and Brinner's results is that the expected rate of inflation rises only part way, to, say, 1½% per year. If that were the actual rate, we would be at point B with no reduction in U. However, the actual rate of inflation is greater than the expected; a gap is created. We move up S'S' to point C. Connecting points such as A and C yields the long-run permanent Phillips curve, LL.

The extension of LL past actual rates of inflation of 2½% is, however, another matter. For according to the authors' results, people's expectations adjust so that the gap between actual and expected inflation rates does not widen. Hence, LL becomes vertical as in Figure 4-4.

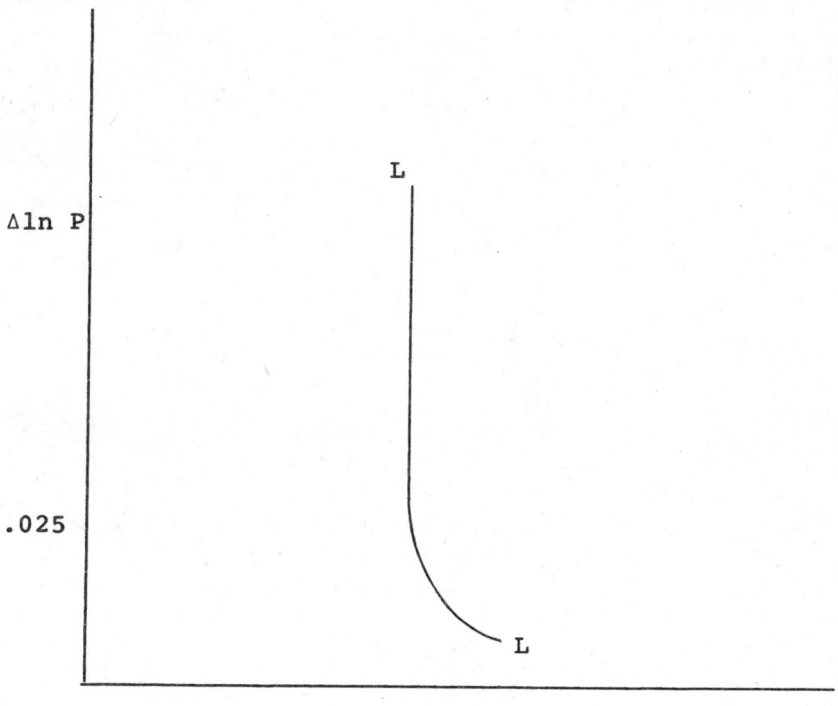

Figure 4-4

III. EXPECTATIONS AND THE PHILLIPS CURVE

We ended the last chapter with the following linear approximation of the relationship between inflation and unemployment, derived from a model of search unemployment:

$$(\Delta \ln P_t^* - \Delta \ln P_t) \cdot 100 = \lambda (Ur - Ur^*) \qquad (4-2)$$

If we rearrange this relationship, we get:

$$(\Delta \ln P_t) \, 100 = (\Delta \ln P_t^*) \, 100 - \lambda (Ur - Ur^*) \qquad (4-3)$$

Equation 4-3 has the characteristics of the Phillips curve relationship, but the actual relationship between unemployment and inflation will depend critically on how inflationary expectations, $\Delta \ln P^*$, are formed. This critical variable was left out of the early Phillips curves which were derived from British and American data. The assumption of a more or less permanent trade-off between inflation and unemployment can be generated by 4-3 only if we assume that the expected rate of inflation does not fully adjust to reality as would be the case, for example, if the first term on the right-hand side of 4-3 never changed. To better understand this, let us take a numerical example.

Assume the following:

(1) $Ur^* = 4.5\%$

(2) $\Delta \ln P_t^* = 0.04$ (annual compounded rate)

(3) $\Delta \ln y_t = 0.04$ (annual compounded rate)

(4) $\lambda = 1$

Given these assumptions, we can see from 4-3 that the rate of growth of nominal aggregate demand would have to be 8% in order to insure full employment. Prices would have to increase at a 4% annual rate while full employment real output increased at a 4% annual rate also. In this manner an annual unemployment rate of 4.5% would obtain. This can be seen by inserting the assumptions 1 through 4 into equation 4-3:

$$100 \, (\Delta \ln P_t) = 100 \, (\Delta \ln P_t^*) - (Ur - Ur^*) \qquad (4-4)$$
$$100 \, (\Delta \ln P_t) = 4\% - (Ur - 4.5\%)$$

Returning now to the simplified aggregate demand model used in the previous chapters, we can determine the annual increase in the stock of money required to insure full employment in this system. Assume for the moment that k, the ratio of desired money balances to nominal income, declines at an annual rate of 2.5%. Then optimal employment (with an unemployment rate = U*) would require an annual increase in the money supply of 5.5%, since:

$$\triangle \ln M - \triangle \ln k = \triangle \ln y_t + \triangle \ln P \qquad (4\text{--}5)$$

Then:

$$\triangle \ln M + 0.025 = \triangle \ln y_t + \triangle \ln P \qquad (4\text{--}6)$$
$$= 0.04 + 0.04 = 0.08$$

Since we assumed that the expected rate of inflation is always 4%, the long-run annual increase in the money supply will determine both the rate of inflation and the unemployment rate. The monetary authorities in this situation would be faced with the dilemma of trading less unemployment for a higher rate of inflation.

In what follows we present further examples using the simplified liquidity preference function. Let us suppose now that the Federal Reserve has been increasing the money supply at 5.5% a year but suddenly decides to reduce the rate of monetary growth to 4.5% in order to bring the rate of inflation below 4%. The annual rate of increase of nominal aggregate demand would automatically slow to 7% per year, since:

$$\triangle \ln M + 0.025 = 0.07 \qquad (4\text{--}7)$$

In the blissful world where the price system produces full employment at each moment in time (the classical full employment world), real output would continue to grow at 4% and the rate of inflation would instantaneously fall to 3%. However, under the assumption of an expected rate of inflation of 4%, the price system cannot instantaneously produce full employment with a new lower actual rate of inflation of 3%. As long as economic decisions are based upon expectations of a continued rate of inflation of 4%, an actual rate of inflation of 3% is inconsistent with full employment. Our Phillips curve relationship indicates that the unemployment rate will rise to 5.5%. In this situation, there is a 1-to-1 trade-off between a reduction in the rate of inflation and an increase in the rate of unemployment.

However, the rate of inflation will not immediately fall to 3%, for an increasing unemployment rate implies a slower growth in output than the potential 4% rate, permitting prices to rise at a rate greater than 3%. When the unemployment rate reaches its steady-state rate of 5.5%, Okun's law (see p. 25) tells us that the price level will be 3% higher and output 3% lower than levels which would have been realized if output had continued to grow at its potential rate of 4%. This can be seen by looking at:

$$Ur_t = 4.5\% + \tfrac{1}{3} (\frac{y_t - y}{y_t}) 100 \qquad (4\text{--}8)$$
$$= 5.5\%$$

Similarly, an increase in the rate of monetary growth to 6.5% would reduce the steady-state unemployment rate to 3.5% and increase the rate of inflation to 5%. The Phillips curve trade-off between unemployment and inflation is indeed a reality in this simplified model. In fact, the trade-off looks permanent, but remember that it rests on some very strong assumptions.

IV. INTRODUCING CHANGING EXPECTATIONS

The permanent trade-off between inflation and unemployment is derived from the assumption of a constant expected rate of inflation. This implies that no one learns from past forecasting errors. In fact, however, past errors in forecasting will modify current forecasts. The simplest notion of adaptive expectations (discussed in more detail in the following chapter) can be formulated in the following manner:

$$(\Delta \ln P^*_t - \Delta \ln P^*_{t-1}) = \delta (\Delta \ln P_{t-1} - \Delta \ln P^*_{t-1}) \qquad (4\text{--}9)$$

This process of forming expectations will produce only a short-run trade-off between inflation and unemployment; no long-run trade-off will exist. This is perhaps best understood by recognizing that in this adaptive expectations model the forecasted values of the rate of change of prices are based on past rates of change of prices.

$$\Delta \ln P_t^* = \delta \sum_{x=0}^{\infty} \Delta \ln P_{t-x} (1-\delta)^x \qquad (4\text{--}10)$$

which becomes:

$$\Delta \ln P_t^* = \delta \Delta \ln P_t + (1-\delta) \Delta \ln P_{t-1}^* \qquad (4\text{--}11)$$

If we are given the past values of inflation which have determined $\Delta \ln P_{t-1}^*$, the monetary authorities can obviously trade less employment for more inflation. In fact, the short-run trade-off implied by this particular adaptive expectations hypothesis is:

$$(\Delta \ln P_t^* - \Delta \ln P_t)\,100 = Ur - 4.5\% \qquad (4\text{--}12)$$
$$= (1-\delta)\,(\Delta \ln P_{t-1}^* - \Delta \ln P_t)\,100$$

Whenever the authorities wish to reduce the unemployment rate below its normal rate (by assumption in this example) of 4.5%, however, the rate of inflation must accelerate. Suppose, for example, that the unemployment rate is to be kept at 3.5%. By equation 4–12, then, we would require that:

$$(\Delta \ln P_t^* - \Delta \ln P_t) = -.01 \qquad (4\text{--}13)$$

But since the adaptive expectations hypothesis assumes that the expected rate of inflation would be increasing in this situation, the actual rate of inflation must accelerate to maintain the gap:

$$(\Delta \ln P_t^* - \Delta \ln P_{t-1}^*) = \delta\,(\Delta \ln P_{t-1} - \Delta \ln P_{t-1}^*)$$
$$= 0.0\delta \qquad (4\text{--}14)$$

Hence, the actual rate of inflation would have to accelerate δ percentage points a year. The rate of inflation in this adaptive expectations model would have to accelerate in order to maintain the trade-off between unemployment and inflation.

This is the so-called *accelerationist* version of the Phillips curve, most notably presented by Phelps and Friedman. In order to maintain an unemployment rate below 4.5% (the normal rate of unemployment) the actual rate of inflation must exceed the expected rate of inflation. But, since expectations eventually adjust toward reality in this particular model, an accelerating rate of inflation is required to maintain the gap between actual and expected wage offers. Consequently, there is no long-run trade-off between inflation and unemployment; only an unanticipated accelerating inflation can maintain an unemployment rate below its equilibrium level.

Basically, then, the successful use of aggregate monetary and fiscal demand policies to control unemployment depends on the stability of a disequilibrium adjustment process such as presented in 4-9 and 4-11. Unanticipated inflation reduces unemployment, but fully anticipated inflation does not. Hence, the extent to which aggregate monetary and fiscal demand policies can affect the unemployment rate depends crucially upon the costs and returns of learning to forecast more accurately, and also the time framework within which individuals observe past behavior and past forecasting mistakes.

Once individuals learn to anticipate the long-run inflationary effects of expansionary monetary or fiscal policies, the adjustment of expectations to reality will be more rapid, reducing the employment effects of aggregate demand policies. Any theory predicting a stable empirical relationship between the unemployment rate and the rate of inflation implies a stable law of disequilibrium price dynamics explaining why individuals make forecasting errors. No such theory could predict the relationship between inflation and unemployment in the long-run, for if individuals understood the theory, they would no longer make the forecasting errors predicted by the theory. There is no stable law of disequilibrium price dynamics, for when decision-makers learn the law, it is no longer descriptive.

SELECTED REFERENCES

1. See text footnotes.
2. Friedman, M., "The Role of Monetary Policy," *American Economic Review*, volume 58, March, 1968, pp. 1–17.
3. Phelps, E.S., "Money Wage Dynamics and Labor Market Equilibrium," *Journal of Political Economy*, volume 76, no. 4, Part II, July/August, 1968.

CHAPTER 5. THE FORMATION OF EXPECTATIONS

To fully understand the relationship between inflation and unemployment, we must develop the rationale for the formulation of the expected rate of inflation. In the last chapter we introduced one model of expectations formation, the adaptive expectations model. In this chapter, we shall discuss in greater detail the rationale for this particular formulation of inflationary expectations and indicate its weakness as a guide to quantitative policy evaluation.

Although until recently the role of expectations was ignored in the analysis of Keynesian macro theory, one need only look to the index of the *General Theory* to find expectation prominent: there is a listing of at least 29 places where the diligent reader can find a mention of expectations. Even before the publication of the *General Theory*, Keynes had referred to "anticipated normal" levels of certain variables in his *Treatise on Money* (New York, 1930, volume 2, p. 137). Essentially, Keynes was referring to the averaging of future anticipated values as the way in which economic agents arrived at some anticipated normal level for any variable under consideration.

I. IRVING FISHER'S RESEARCH ON EXPECTATIONS FORMATION

In his *Theory of Interest*, published in 1930, the American economist Irving Fisher posited the basic formulation of an expectations model which has been widely used in the last several decades in the United States for econometric research. His empirical research indicated that current expectations of inflation are a weighted average of past rates of inflation. More specifically, Fisher's specification of the formulation of expectations made the expected rate of inflation a distributed lag function of past rates of inflation with the most recent observations of inflation most heavily weighted. Fisher's expectations model leads to the conclusion that individuals will underestimate the current rate of inflation if inflation is accelerating. In a separate context, he recognized the implications of this forecasting bias for the trade-off between inflation and unemployment as early as 1926 in his article, "A Statistical Relation between Unemployment and Price Changes." [1]

II. RECENT DEVELOPMENTS IN ADAPTIVE EXPECTATIONS MODELS

The adaptive expectations model was not widely used in econometric research until the pioneering studies of Koyck on capacity adjustment, Cagen on the demand for cash balances during hyper-inflation, Friedman on the consumption function, and Nerlove on agriculture supply functions. The basic decision rule of the adaptive expectations model can be illustrated in the following manner: The economic agent—let us say, the individual worker—is attempting to predict the rate of inflation ($\triangle \ln P_t^*$) with knowledge of the rate of inflation in the past period ($\triangle \ln P_{t-1}$). The adaptive expectations model hypothesizes that expectations are revised in *proportion* to the forecast error associated with the last period's expectations of inflation, or:

$$\triangle \ln P_t^* = \triangle \ln P_{t-1}^* + \lambda \left\{ \triangle \ln P_{t-1} - \ln P_{t-1}^* \right\} \qquad (5\text{–}1)$$

This can be simplified so that the expected rate of inflation is a geometrically declining distributed lag function of all past rates of inflation. This can be shown by changing 5–1 into:

$$\triangle \ln P_t^* = \lambda \triangle \ln P_{t-1} + (1-\lambda) \triangle \ln P_{t-1}^* \qquad (5\text{–}2)$$

Similarly:

$$\triangle \ln P_{t-1}^* = \lambda \triangle \ln P_{t-2} + (1-\lambda) \triangle \ln P_{t-2}^* \qquad (5\text{–}3)$$

and so forth. After repeated iterations we will obtain the following:

$$\triangle \ln P_t^* = \lambda \sum_{i=1}^{\infty} (1-\lambda)^{i-1} \triangle \ln P_{t-1} \qquad (5\text{–}4)$$

---

[1]. *International Labour Review*, 13, no. 6, June, 1926, pp. 785–792.

In other words, the formulation of the expectation of the rate of change of prices tomorrow is based on a geometrically declining weighted average of all past rates of change of prices. Depending on what λ is, more or less weight will be given to the most recent rates of change of prices. At one extreme, if λ is equal to 1:

$$\Delta \ln P^*_{t+1} = \Delta \ln P_t \qquad (5\text{-}4')$$

This is commonly referred to as a no-change extrapolation model. At the other extreme, as λ approaches zero, more and more weight is given to values of the rate of change of prices further and further in the past.

The adaptive expectations model has been extremely useful in empirical studies and numerous authors have come up with alternative justifications for its use. For example, Arrow and Nerlove justified its use by saying:

> Past and present prices reflect forces which determine the level about which future prices may be expected to fluctuate: the more recent the past price the more it expresses the operation of those forces relevant to expectation.[2]

It is obvious from the onset that the adaptive expectations model seems to imply that individuals never learn, or in the words of Mills:

> . . . in the adaptive expectations model, expectations are not only always wrong whenever the market is out of equilibrium, but they are always wrong in a very simple and systematic way. Presumably an intelligent decision-maker would be able to observe such biases in his expectations and would refrain from using the method by which such expectations were formed.[3]

III. FURTHER JUSTIFICATION OF ADAPTIVE EXPECTATIONS MODEL

The exponentially weighted moving average forecast in equation 5-4 has certain optimal properties which further rationalize its use as a model of expectations formation in certain situa-

---

2. Arrow, K. J., and M. Nerlove, "A Note on Expectations and Stability," *Econometrica*, April, 1958, volume 26, p. 298.

3. Mills, E. S., "The Use of Adaptive Expectations in Stability Analysis: Comment," *Quarterly Journal of Economics*, May, 1961, volume 75, pp. 322-333.

tions. John Muth[4] demonstrated that an exponentially weighted average of past rates of inflation can be interpreted as the expected value of the present rate of inflation if the underlying inflation-generating function is a random walk with noise superimposed. This inflation-generating function is basically of the following form:

$$\Delta \ln P_t = \pi_t + U_t \tag{5-5}$$

π_t is interpreted here as a permanent random component (not necessarily with a mean of zero) representing the "true" change in the rate of inflation resulting from shifts in monetary and fiscal policy actions. U_t is a transitory random component representing random disturbances lasting for only one period. These transitory random disturbances are the "noise" generated by the stochastic nature of aggregate demand. This noise generated by the transitory component, U_t, makes it difficult to perceive the movements in π_t.

Muth demonstrated that the forecasting model which minimizes the error variance (the expected value of $[\Delta \ln P_t - \Delta \ln P_t^*]^2$) has the form of an exponentially weighted distributed lag such as:

$$\Delta \ln P_t^* = \lambda \sum_{i=1}^{\infty} (1-\lambda)^{i-1} \Delta \ln P_{t-1} \tag{5-6}$$

In simple terms, the justification for use of an exponentially weighted moving average to forecast inflation generated by equation 5-5 is that it corrects forecasts in the presence of persistent errors introduced by the permanent component π_t, but it doesn't respond very much to the transitory component U_t. If the variance of π_t is large relative to the variance of U_t, the optimal λ will be close to one; that is, most of the weight will be given to the most recent rates of inflation. On the other hand, if the variance of U_t is large relative to the variance of π_t, the optimal λ will be close to zero. If λ were close to zero, equal weights would be given to all past rates of inflation.

4. Muth, John, "Optimal Properties of Exponentially Weighted Forecasts," *Journal of American Statistical Association*, vol. 55 (June, 1960).

IV. OTHER VERSIONS OF THE MODEL

As an aside, the random walk model has been applied with great success in stock market analyses (see especially Cootner) and also, surprisingly enough, in analyzing the stochastic structure of the velocity of money. J. P. Gould and C. R. Nelson, for example, conclude that the velocity series constructed by Friedman and Schwartz "is well characterized as a simple random walk."[5] Further, "the simple random walk model yields better post-sample predictions than either a random-walk-with drift model or a constant-velocity model". The fact that the velocity series appears *ex post* to have nonrandom patterns and trends is not actually inconsistent with the hypotheses that the series is a random walk. For these apparent trends appear in random walk series in physics, education, economics, and many other fields. What is important to note is that a random walk process will exhibit no affinity for any particular mean level or for any particular trend. Rather, it will display ever increasingly large departures from any given level or any given trend line as time progresses. A more detailed analysis of the random walk hypothesis, when applied to both monetarist and Keynesian alternative frameworks for analyzing macroeconomic activity shows, according to Gould and Nelson, that most, if not all, can be reconciled with the hypothesis that velocity has a random walk.

There are more sophisticated versions of 5-1. For example, Allais[6] suggests that the coefficient of adaptive adjustment, λ, should itself be a function of the past rates of change in the price level. Basically, Allais indicates that λ will be larger the greater the most recent rates of change in prices. In other words, economic agents will be more sensitive to current data in such a situation. However, it does not appear that Allais' specification of the adaptive expectations model will allow it to be used for policy purposes in order for the monetary and fiscal authorities to alter the rate of unemployment. The Phillips curve trade-off, remember, is based on biased predictions of the rate of change of prices by workers in the economy. In using Allais' formulation of 5-1, where λ is itself a function of past rates of change of prices, the monetary and fiscal authorities would still be faced with the possibility that merely altering the rate of

---

5. "The Stochastic Structure of the Velocity of Money, *AER* (June, 1974).

6. Maurice Allais, "A Restatement of the Quantity Theory of Money," *American Economic Review*, volume 61, December, 1966, pp. 1123–1157.

acceleration in prices in order to fool people and, hence, induce biased expectations, ignores the fact that persons will eventually learn. Once the monetary and fiscal authorities attempt to calculate how the economy reacts to the pattern of past data in order to make policy for the future, rational individuals will eventually learn and adjust their own price formulations to incorporate this new knowledge—the new policy will be ineffective as a means of reducing the rate of unemployment. We are right back where we started. There is no stable law of disequilibrium price dynamics.

Furthermore, Muth's analysis indicates that rational individuals would use the adaptive expectations model to form unbiased forecasts as long as the underlying inflation-generating function were a random walk as in equation 5-5. The assumption of rational behavior implies that policy-makers could not use a Phillips curve model such as equation 4-2 to "control" the unemployment rate. The Phillips curve trade-off, remember, is based on *biased* predictions of the rate of inflation by workers in the economy. If policy-makers used the adaptive expectations model to "control" the unemployment rate in any systematic way, the adaptive expectations model would yield *biased* forecasts. It would no longer be "rational" to use the adaptive expectations model to forecast the rate of inflation. Eventually rational individuals will modify their forecasting equation to produce unbiased estimates and the predictive ability of the policy model will be destroyed. Once the monetary and fiscal authorities base policy decisions on how the economy reacts in disequilibrium, rational individuals will eventually learn and adjust their decision rules, destroying the predictive content of the policy-maker's model. Robert Lucas puts it this way:

> Given that (1) the structure of an econometric model consists of optimal decision rules of economic agents, and that (2) optimal decision rules vary systematically with changes in the structure of series relevant to the decision maker; it follows that (3) any change in policy will systematically alter the structure of econometric models.[7]

7. Lucas, "Econometric Policy Evaluation: A Critique," at Conference on the Phillips Curve, Center for Research in Government Policy and Business, April 20, 21, 1973, University of Rochester.

V. USING A MODEL TO FORM EXPECTATIONS

Individual decision-makers could construct their own macro-models. The models predict on the basis of exogenous variables such as the money supply or fiscal actions which *determine* future wages and prices. If individuals could immediately make unbiased forecasts of wages and prices from current shifts in monetary and fiscal policy, policy-makers could not affect employment. Changes in aggregate demand would merely change nominal wages and prices as in the classical demand-pull inflation model.

VI. DIRECT CONTROLS

The inherent difficulties of using monetary and fiscal actions to "control" the unemployment rate have contributed to the evolution of employment policies which influence expectations by direct wage and price controls. For example, the 90-day wage and price freeze of August 15, 1971 was implemented, according to the Council of Economic Advisors, "to reestablish an acceptably low rate of price increase by reducing expectations of continued strong inflation and eliminating, to the extent possible, practices and behavior which sustain or promote inflation." [8] They further state that "the basic premise of the price-wage control system is that the inflation of 1970–71 was the result of expectations, contracts, and patterns of behavior built up during the earlier period, beginning in 1965, when there was an inflationary excessive demand . . . The purpose of the control system is to give the country a period of enforced stability in which expectations, contracts, and behavior will become adapted to the fact that rapid inflation is no longer the prospective condition of the American way of life." [9]

In chapter 8 we shall discuss in greater detail the subject of wage and price controls.

SELECTED REFERENCES
See footnotes and Selected References, Chapter 3.

8. *Report of the President's Council of Economic Advisors*, 1972, p. 83.
9. *Ibid.*, p. 108.

CHAPTER 6. THE EMPLOYMENT AND PRICE EFFECTS OF LABOR MARKET RESTRICTIONS

In the late 1950s, numerous economists such as Sumner Slichter attributed "creeping inflation" to attempts by organized labor to increase their share of national income. Wage increases in excess of labors' productivity increases were considered a major element producing inflation. The argument that labor unions have been a principal source of inflationary pressure seems to be contradicted, however, by the following evidence. Less of the labor force is unionized here than in most industrial countries. Sweden and Britain can both boast that more than 40 percent of their labor force is unionized. On the other hand, only 22 percent of the U. S. labor force belongs to organized labor.

Back in 1953, 26 percent of our labor force was unionized. This figure fell to about 24 percent for the rest of the fifties. Then by 1961 it was almost 23 percent and has fallen gradually since. The reasons for such a reversed trend in unionization of the U. S. labor force are many, but several stand out. There has been a rapid growth in the service (or tertiary) sector of the economy. It has been very difficult for unions to organize in the services. Today less than 10 percent of all service workers belong to unions.

In addition, much of the gain in manufacturing employment has involved increased white-collar employment. Only about 15 percent of all white-collar workers are in unions.

The argument that union power contributes to inflation ignores the possibility that increases in union wages may cause nonunion wages to fall. Institutional labor market restrictions may have their principal effect on the structure of wages, rather than on their absolute level.

This chapter discusses microeconomic aspects of labor market restrictions, principally those caused by union collective bargaining and minimum wage restrictions.

I. UNION COLLECTIVE BARGAINING

The public sometimes looks at collective bargaining as if labor and management were merely haggling over labor's share of business revenue. This analytic approach misleadingly assumes that workers can receive higher wages without anyone else receiving less except the employer. However, if a union succeeds in raising wage rates above the competitive level, either the owners of complimentary productive resources (usually capital investments in the industry) or the consumer will pay the bill.

The degree to which a complimentary productive resource bears the burden of the higher labor costs depends upon the ease with which it can be transferred to an alternative use. Any productive resource with an upward sloping supply schedule earns economic rent. The intra-marginal supply of resources will continue to produce even though earnings fall. The ability to transfer capital out of the unionized industry will increase its elasticity of supply to the industry. Obviously, those productive resources which are fixed in supply (sunk investments) will bear most of the burden of higher wages.

The owners of fixed assets (railroad track and steel mills, for example) are particularly vulnerable to aggressive union wage policies. Once those fixed investments are made, it is extremely difficult to transfer them to other uses. Investors expect, of course, to earn the market rate of return (for the risk class) over the lifetime of the capital investment. Once the capital investment is made, though, the investor must accept the residual which is left after paying labor and other costs, since the investment is "sunk."

To the extent that higher wages reduce the earnings of fixed investment (i. e., reduce rents), there will be no reduction in consumer surplus. Ultimately, however, higher wages will raise prices because new investment expenditures will not occur if investors expect to earn less than the market rate of return for that risk class. That is, without new investment, the supply of the product will eventually be restricted, raising prices and reducing consumer surplus. Prices will continue to rise until new investment becomes profitable. Output, of course, will be reduced as consumers will desire to purchase less at higher prices. Employment will then fall, even if there is no factor substitution.

This *employment effect* of union wage policies divides the self interest of the beneficiaries of the higher wages from the self interest of those workers who otherwise could have been employed in the industry. This lack of unanimity of interest among employees ultimately limits the union's organizational strength. Unions are best able to maintain unanimity of self interest in bargaining for higher wages if industry employment is rapidly increasing. Most employment losses would then be at the expense of potential future employees rather than at the expense of current union members. Among industries with the same growth potential, those industries with the least elastic demand schedules for union labor will be the most attractive prospects for relatively high wage policies by labor unions. The more inelastic the demand schedule for labor, the smaller will be the employment loss from a given increase in wage rates.

The demand schedule for labor will be more inelastic as (1) the supply schedules of complimentary factors of production are inelastic, (2) the demand schedule for output is inelastic and (3) the elasticity of factor substitution is low.

To facilitate examining the first condition in more detail, assume that there is no factor substitution. The earnings of sunk investments are not costs to the industry. With no factor substitution, unions could raise wages to the point where all the economic rent earned by sunk investments is absorbed by labor costs without reducing employment or raising prices. However, even in this situation the employment level cannot be maintained in the long run. The income earned by sunk investment is a quasi-rent, for additional investment would be required to maintain (or increase) the capital stock. In the long run, that income is a cost, because new investment will take place only if investors expect it to earn the risk-corrected market rate of return. As the capital stock depreciates, employment and output will fall.

Industries with large sunk investments in highly durable assets make excellent prospects for labor monopolies because of the possible transfer of the quasi-rents of sunk investments to wage income.[1] In industries with little sunk investment, the short-run demand for labor schedule will tend to be more elastic. Capital investments in those industries could be transferred

---

1. It is also true that these industries are highly capital intensive. Thus labor's share is very small. Effects of union on prices would hence also be relatively small.

quickly to other sectors of the economy where higher earnings are possible. The shorter the durability of the asset, the more rapidly sunk investments depreciate if replacement is not profitable. Even the potential threat of high wage policies by labor unions increases the risk associated with investment in highly durable fixed assets. Investors would require a higher expected rate of return on new investment to compensate for the risk associated with labor union monopoly power.

In many industries, of course, employers can adapt to higher wage rates by substituting labor saving capital equipment for union labor. If wage rates are $2.00 an hour, it is not profitable to use equipment which costs the firm $2,500 a year and saves only 1,000 man-hours of labor a year. Let the wage rate increase to $3.00 an hour, though, and the firm will find it profitable to replace labor with capital equipment. Although fixed factor coefficients of production may be common in the short run, in the long run different production technologies can be used. Higher wage rates commonly accelerate the introduction of labor-saving, automated machinery. In a sense, one kind of labor is substituted for another type of labor since the cost of labor-saving machinery consists mainly of the labor costs of producing it. One distinction worth noting, however, is that savings are absorbed by the purchase of the labor-saving machinery because it embodies a stream of services which replace labor services now and in the future. Although union induced wage premiums artificially stimulate new investment in labor-saving equipment, they may not increase the productivity of labor in general because the investment diverts savings from other investment projects.

In order to better understand the concepts just presented, we now construct a formal partial equilibrium model of the derived demand for labor.

II. DEMAND FOR LABOR

The formal demand for labor schedule can be conceptualized as consisting of a factor substitution effect and a scale effect. Assume that the industry's production function is linear homogeneous (constant returns to scale), as represented in Figure 6–1. Minimum cost conditions would occur at the tangency of the

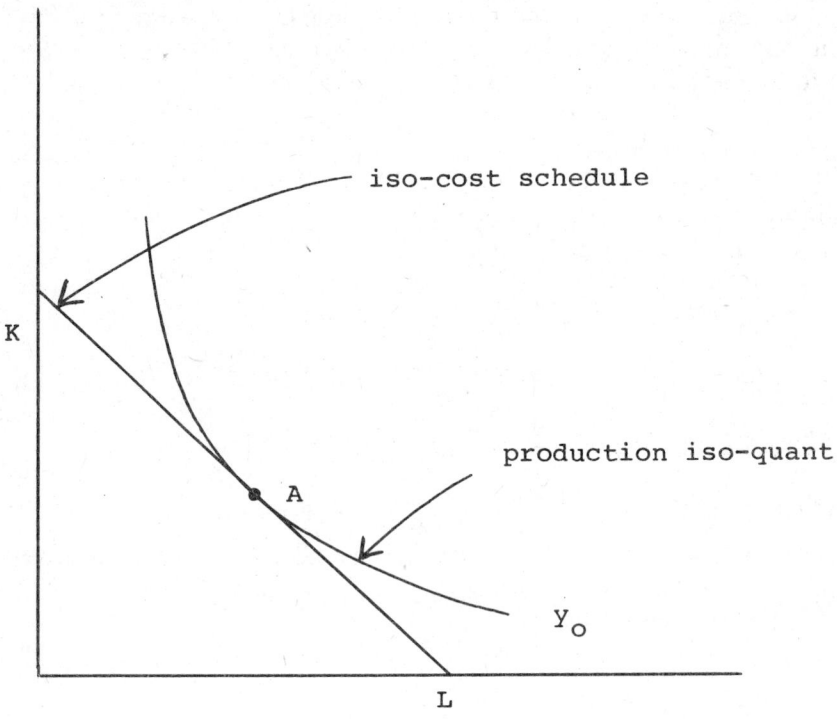

Figure 6-1

Production Function of the Industry [A8683]

iso-cost line and the production iso-quant, or point A. The slope of the production iso-quant at any point is equal to:

$$-\frac{\text{marginal product of labor services}}{\text{marginal product of capital services}} = -\frac{MPL}{MPK} \quad (6\text{–}1)$$

The slope of the iso-cost schedule is:

$$-\frac{w}{r} \quad (6\text{–}2)$$

where r = rental rate for the stream of capital services
w = wage rate

Consequently, the minimum cost condition occurs

where $\dfrac{MPL}{MPK} = \dfrac{w}{r}$.

The static long-run rental rate of capital services is equal to the sum market rate of interest for risk class plus depreciation rate times the purchase price of the capital asset:

$$r = (i + d) P_K$$

where i = market rate of interest

d = rate of depreciation (capital gains are treated as negative depreciation)

P_K = purchase price of the capital asset

For linear homogeneous production functions, the $\frac{K}{L}$ ratio, which minimizes the cost of any given level of production, depends only on $\frac{r}{w}$. This condition can be summarized in terms of the production function's elasticity of substitution:

$$S = \frac{\frac{d(K/L)}{K/L}}{\frac{d(r/w)}{r/w}} \qquad (6\text{--}3)$$

The scale effect relates unit costs and demand for final output. Perfect competition requires total revenue to be equal to total costs, or

$$yP = rK + wL \qquad (6\text{--}4)$$

where y = output

P = price of final output

K = quantity of capital services

L = quantity of labor services

The own price elasticity of demand holding all other prices constant (E) is defined as:

$$E = \frac{dy/y}{dP/P} \qquad (6\text{--}5)$$

Since price is equal to average per unit cost under the assumption of perfect competition, the percentage increase in price can be specified as:

$$\frac{dP}{P} = FL\frac{dw}{w} + FK\frac{dr}{r} \qquad (6\text{--}6)$$

where FL = labor's share of total costs

FK = capital's share of total costs

Therefore, the percentage increase in output demanded is:

$$\frac{dy}{y} = E\left\{FL\frac{dw}{w} + FK\frac{dr}{r}\right\} \qquad (6\text{--}7)$$

The supply schedule is derived from the marginal productivity conditions at the equilibrium point:

$$\frac{dy}{y} = \left(\frac{dK}{K}\right)\frac{MPK}{APK} + \left(\frac{dL}{L}\right)\frac{MPL}{APL} \qquad (6\text{--}8)$$

where APK = average product of capital services

APL = average produce of labor services

If producers are price takers, the maximization of profits requires that:

$$r = MPK \cdot P \qquad (6\text{--}9)$$

and

$$w = MPL \cdot P \qquad (6\text{--}10)$$

Therefore:

$$\frac{MPK}{APK} = \frac{r/P}{y/K} = \frac{rK}{yP} = FK \qquad (6\text{--}11)$$

and

$$\frac{MPL}{APL} = \frac{w/P}{y/L} = \frac{wL}{yP} = FL \qquad (6\text{--}12)$$

The demand for labor schedule can then be derived from the simultaneous solution of the following three equations:

Elasticity of substitution:

$$S\left(\frac{dr}{r} - \frac{dw}{w}\right) = \frac{dK}{K} - \frac{dL}{L} \qquad (6\text{--}13)$$

Demand schedule for final output:

$$\frac{dy}{y} = E\left(FL\frac{dw}{w} + FK\frac{dr}{r}\right) \qquad (6\text{-}14)$$

Supply schedule:

$$\frac{dy}{y} = FL\frac{dL}{L} + FK\frac{dK}{K} \qquad (6\text{-}15)$$

A. DERIVED DEMAND FOR LABOR WHEN CAPITAL SUPPLY IS PERFECTLY ELASTIC

If the supply of capital to the industry is perfectly elastic, dr/r is equal to zero. This condition is approximated in the long run when we can assume that capital investments are transferred to alternative uses, making the actual rate of return on capital in the industry equal to the market rate of return, which is considered constant.

When $dr/r = 0$, the demand for labor schedule is derived from the following equations:

$$-S\frac{dw}{w} = -\frac{dL}{L} + \frac{dK}{K} \qquad (6\text{-}16)$$

and

$$E\left(FL\frac{dw}{w}\right) = FL\frac{dL}{L} + FK\frac{dK}{K} \qquad (6\text{-}17)$$

The simultaneous solution is:

$$\frac{\frac{dL}{L}}{\frac{dw}{w}} = S\,FK + FL\,E$$

(both S and E are negative).

B. DEMAND FOR LABOR WHEN CAPITAL SUPPLY IS PERFECTLY INELASTIC

If we assume that the capital stock is fixed, on the other hand, then $\frac{dK}{K} = 0$. This approximates a short-run situation where capital investment is sunk. Since the capital stock cannot be transferred to alternative uses, the rental rate is a quasi-rent. The demand for labor would then be derived from the following equations:

$$S\left(\frac{dr}{r} - \frac{dw}{w}\right) = -\frac{dL}{L} \tag{6-19}$$

$$E\left(FL\frac{dw}{w} + FK\frac{dr}{r}\right) = FL\frac{dL}{L} \tag{6-20}$$

The simultaneous solution is:

$$\frac{\frac{dL}{L}}{\frac{dw}{w}} = \frac{ES}{F_L S + F_K E} \tag{6-21}$$

Consequently, if the capital stock is fixed and the elasticity of substitution is zero, the elasticity of the demand for labor is zero. Labor could capture all the quasi-rents going to such investment without any loss of employment in the short run.

C. THE MORE GENERAL CASE

In general, $\frac{dK}{K} = \frac{dr}{r}\varepsilon$, where $\varepsilon =$ the elasticity of supply of capital to the industry. Substituting $\frac{dr}{r}\varepsilon$ for $\frac{dK}{K}$ in equations 6–13, 6–14, and 6–15, we get:

$$S\left(\frac{dr}{r} - \frac{dw}{w}\right) = \frac{dK}{K} - \frac{dL}{L} \tag{6-22}$$

and

$$E\left(\frac{dw}{w}FL + \frac{dr}{r}FK\right) = FL\frac{dL}{L} + FK\frac{dK}{K} \tag{6-23}$$

which become:

$$S\left(\frac{dr}{r} - \frac{dw}{w}\right) = \varepsilon\frac{dr}{r} - \frac{dL}{L} \tag{6-24}$$

$$E\left(\frac{dw}{w}FL + \frac{dr}{r}FK\right) = FL\frac{dL}{L} + FK\varepsilon\frac{dr}{r} \tag{6-25}$$

The simultaneous solution is:

$$\frac{\frac{dL}{L}}{\frac{dw}{w}} = \frac{(\varepsilon - S)\ E\ FL + FK\ S\ (\varepsilon - E)}{(\varepsilon - S)\ FL + FK\ (\varepsilon - E)} \qquad (6\text{--}26)$$

A few empirical estimates of these various elasticities will now be presented.

III. EMPIRICAL EXAMPLES OF THE DERIVED DEMAND FOR LABOR

H. Gregg Lewis [2] used the long-run model 6–18 to estimate the employment effects of United Mine Worker wage policies during the 1950s. In 1945 bituminous coal miners received wages approximately equal to the average wage in manufacturing. By 1959, hourly earnings were 28% higher than in manufacturing and hourly compensation was 42% higher. Man-hours of employment declined by 75% and man-days declined by 60% in the period 1947–1961. Some of that employment decline was a result of the declining demand for coal. Lewis estimated, 6–3, the elasticity of factor substitution (S) in the bituminous coal industry to be about –1. Since the labor factor share (FL) was about 50% of total costs, Lewis estimated that the substitution effect was responsible for a 21% decline in man-hours of employment by 1961.[3] In addition to the substitution effect, higher production costs will eventually raise prices and reduce sales.[4] The use of automated machinery can only partially offset the increase in wage costs. The demand for coal, however, is very inelastic. If, as Lewis assumes in his analysis, the price elasticity is –0.25, a 21% increase in price will reduce sales by only 5¼%. Since labor costs in the bituminous coal industry were about one-half of total costs, a 42% increase in hourly compensation would raise total average costs by only 21%. Consequently, the employment loss from reduced sales would be 5¼% at most. Hence, the total employment loss from the 42% increase in hourly compensation was about 26% in man-hours of labor.

---

2. H. Gregg Lewis, "Relative Employment Effects of Unions," *American Economic Review*/Supplement, volume 54, May, 1964.

3. This substitution effect is the term S FK in equation 6–18.

4. This scale effect is the term FL E in equation 6–18.

IV. EMPLOYER COLLUSION

The extraordinarily large wage increases in the bituminous coal industry during the 1950s may actually have benefitted some large coal operators in the industry by putting labor-intensive coal operators out of business. Wide-stream coal deposits are well suited to the use of capital intensive methods of production. Moreover, the relative scarcity of wide-stream deposits protects the capital intensive operators from new entrants.

In a Supreme Court case (UMW v. Pennington [5]) in 1965, the owners of the Phillips Brothers Coal Company maintained that the National Bituminous Coal Wage Agreement of 1950 was a collusive arrangement by which capital-intensive coal operators joined with the United Mine Workers to disadvantage labor-intensive coal operators. The Supreme Court ruled that unions forfeit their exemption from antitrust laws if they conspire with one set of employers to eliminate competitors from the industry. The Supreme Court then remanded the case to a District Court which failed to find sufficient evidence of actual conspiracy.

Where firms of differing labor intensities compete in the same industry, higher industry-wide wage rates will increase production costs most in the more labor intensive firms; an increase in wage rates throughout the industry will put labor-intensive firms at a competitive disadvantage. If the labor-intensive firms go out of business, the capital-intensive firms may profit from higher prices. In these situations the capital intensive firms may actually encourage collective bargaining agreements which raise wage rates uniformly throughout the industry.

Both groups will suffer, however, if the industry's output does not fall. Prices will not increase unless output falls. In this case, the increased labor costs must be absorbed by those complimentary factors of production which are in fixed supply. The capital-intensive firms will benefit from their cost advantage only if the labor-intensive firms go out of business. Costs have no effect on prices unless they reduce output. However, if the increased labor costs cannot be absorbed by complimentary factors of production which earn economic rents in the labor-intensive firms, they will go out of business, reducing the industry's output and raising prices.

---

5. For an excellent analysis of this case, see Oliver Williamson, "Wage Rates as a Barrier to Entry: The Pennington Case in Perspective," *Quarterly Journal of Economics*, February, 1968.

For example, assume:
1. no factor substitution is possible ($S = 0$),
2. no factor earns economic rent, and
3. other factor prices are constant.

Production costs would then increase in proportion to the firm's labor intensity.

$$\frac{dC_x}{C_x} = FL_x \frac{dw}{w} \qquad (6\text{-}27)$$

$$\frac{dC_y}{C_y} = FL_y \frac{dw}{w} \qquad (6\text{-}28)$$

where C = costs
  w = wage rate
  FL = labor's share of total cost
  subscripts x and y refer to the relative capital-intensive and labor-intensive firms respectively

The potential increase in the price of final output when the labor-intensive firms go out of business ($\frac{dP^*}{P}$) can be derived from the demand schedule. For instance, consider a constant elasticity demand schedule where:

$$E = \frac{dq/q}{dP/P} \qquad (6\text{-}29)$$

where E = price elasticity of demand for the industry's product
  q = output
  P = the price of output

Therefore,

$$\frac{dP^*}{P} = \frac{-x}{E} \qquad (6\text{-}30)$$

where x = the proportion of the industry's output produced by the labor-intensive firms

Given equations 6-28 and 6-30, wage rates must rise sufficiently to increase the costs of the labor-intensive firms more than prices to prevent them from attempting to remain in business. Therefore, wages must rise by at least $\left[-\frac{x}{E} \frac{1}{FL_y} \right]$ to raise costs in the labor-intensive firms by more than prices. (If wages rise by less than $\left[-\frac{x}{E} \frac{1}{FL_y} \right]$, some production by labor-intensive firms would still be profitable. Of course, how output would be rationed among the labor-intensive firms in this situation is indeterminant.) An increase in wage rates of $\left[-\frac{x}{E} \frac{1}{FL_y} \right]$ would raise the price-to-unit cost ratio of the capital intensive firms by:

$$\frac{dP^*}{P} - \frac{dC_x}{C_x} = \frac{dP^*}{P} - FL_x \frac{dw}{w} = \frac{-x}{E} - FL_x \frac{-x}{E\,FL_y}$$

$$= (FL_y - FL_x) \frac{-x}{E\,FL_y} \qquad (6\text{--}31)$$

Equation 6–31 shows that whenever firms within an industry differ significantly in their labor-intensities, and the price elasticity of demand for final output is relatively inelastic, there are substantial incentives for the capital-intensive firms to support industry-wide wage increases.

Of course, the higher profit margins will encourage the capital-intensive firms to expand output and new capital-intensive firms will enter the industry if possible. The entry of new capital-intensive firms will eventually eliminate the excess profits earned by the original capital-intensive firms.

V. WELFARE EFFECTS OF WAGE DIFFERENTIALS

Since wage rates, in competitive equilibrium, reflect the value of labor's marginal product (VLMP) in other industries (assuming producers are price- and wage-takers), the wage differential between the union and nonunion sectors implies that resources are misallocated. The value of output produced by the total labor force would increase if labor were transferred from the nonunion sector to the unionized sector because initially the marginal rate of substitution in consumption is not the same as the marginal rate of substitution in production. Employers in the unionized sector, however, cannot profitably employ additional labor at the union's wage level.

A graphical analysis will more clearly show the above. Figure 6–2 shows the VLMP schedule in the organized sector as a func-

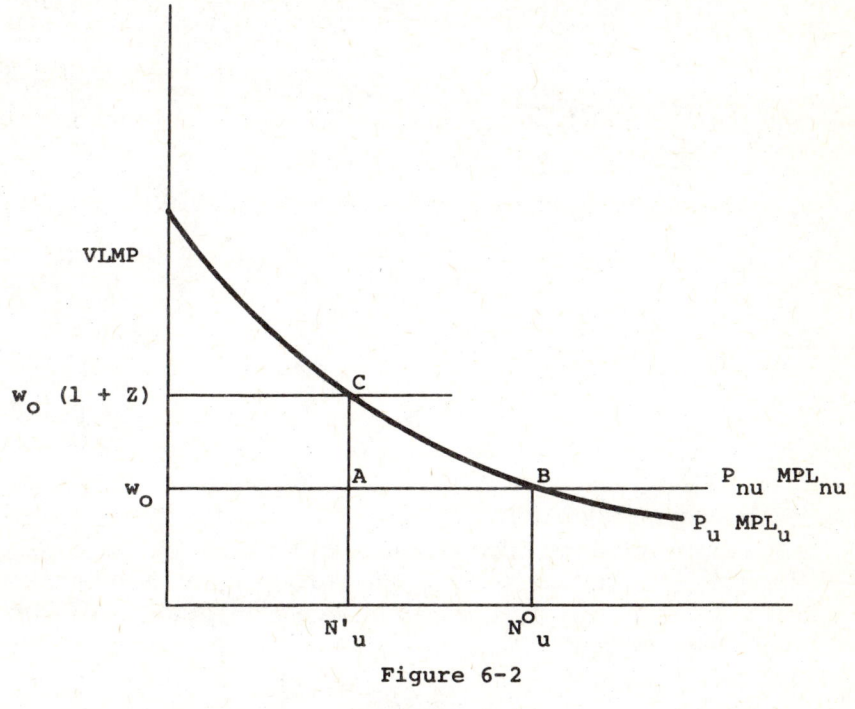

Figure 6-2

VLMP Schedules

(Z = the percentage union wage premium)

tion of union employment. We use the following definition:

$$\text{VLMP}_u = P_u \cdot \text{MPL}_u \qquad (6\text{–}32)$$

$$\text{VLMP}_{nu} = P_{nu} \cdot \text{MPL}_{nu} \qquad (6\text{–}33)$$

where P = price of the final product

MPL = marginal product of labor

subscripts u and nu refer to the unionized and nonunionized sectors, respectively

If we assume that VLMP_{nu} is constant, area ABC is the estimate of the economic value lost through the misallocation of resources. This is the integral of $(\text{VLMP}_u - \text{VLMP}_{nu})$ over the employment loss resulting from the union wage premium.

The welfare loss in Figure 6–2 can be approximated by:

$$WL = \tfrac{1}{2} Z w_o \Delta N_u$$

$$= \tfrac{1}{2} Z \frac{\Delta N_u}{N^o_u} (w_o N^o_u)$$

$$= \tfrac{1}{2} Z^2 \eta_d (w_o N^o_u) \qquad (6\text{–}34)$$

where Z = percentage union wage premium
η_d = elasticity of the demand for labor schedule (VLMP schedule) in the unionized sector
$w_o N^o_u$ = total wage bill if there were no wage premium.

VI. GENERAL EQUILIBRIUM CONSIDERATIONS

In the short run, unionized labor may capture the quasi-rents of sunk investments through increasing their wage premiums without raising the relative price of their product or reducing union employment if no factor substitution is possible. Eventually, however, depreciation of the capital invested in the unionized sector and incentives to substitute other factors for unionized labor will reduce the relative employment of unionized labor. The relative price of union-made products must rise until the rate of return on new investment in the unionized sector is high enough relative to other investment opportunities to prevent the continued reduction of relative employment of union labor.

Johnson and Mieszkowski analyze the distribution effects of wage differentials using a two factor, two sector general equilibrium model.[6] The model assumes that labor and capital are transferred between the two sectors until the rate of return on capital in both sectors is equal. The extent to which nonunion wages are reduced in absorbing workers from the unionized sector depends critically upon the relative labor intensities in the two sectors. Nonunion wages will fall less the greater is the relative labor intensity of the nonunion product. For the United States, however, the construction, manufacturing, transportation, public utilities, communications, and mining industries which were 52% unionized on average in 1953 are labor-intensive relative to the agriculture, crude petroleum, trade, finance, real

---

6. H. G. Johnson and P. Mieszkowski, "The Effects of Unionism on the Distribution of Income: A General Equilibrium Approach," *The Quarterly Journal of Economics*, volume XXXIV, no. 14, November, 1970, pp. 539–561.

estate, and services industries which were only 6% unionized on average in 1953. As a result, the fall in nonunion wages resulting from higher union wages is substantial.

After obtaining several estimates of production and demand parameters, Johnson and Mieszkowski estimate that most, if not all, of the gains of union labor are made at the expense of nonunion labor and not at the expense of aggregate earnings on capital. At one extreme, 77% of union wage gains were at the expense of nonunion labor. At the other extreme, all of union labor wage gains were at the expense of nonunion labor's wages.

A. A TWO SECTOR GENERAL EQUILIBRIUM MODEL OF UNION WAGE POLICIES

The partial equilibrium model developed in the previous sections can readily be extended to a two sector general equilibrium model. The capital stock and the labor force are assumed to be constant so that:

$$dK_x + dK_y = 0 \qquad (6\text{--}35)$$

$$dL_x + dL_y = 0 \qquad (6\text{--}36)$$

(The subscripts refer to the x or y sectors of the economy.) If we consider a time period long enough to permit the transfer of capital from one sector to the other, the rate of return on capital in both sectors will be equal. The production functions in both sectors are assumed to be linear homogeneous and all producers are price-takers.

The demand for the output, q, in the unionized sector x is specified as:

$$\frac{dq_x}{q_x} = E \left(\frac{dP_x}{P_x} - \frac{dP_y}{P_y} \right) \qquad (6\text{--}37)$$

$$\frac{dP_x}{P_x} = FL_x \left(\frac{dw}{w} + dZ \right) + FK_x \left(\frac{dr}{r} \right) \qquad (6\text{--}38)$$

$$\frac{dP_y}{P_y} = FL_y \left(\frac{dw}{w} \right) + FK_y \left(\frac{dr}{r} \right) \qquad (6\text{--}39)$$

where Z = the percentage wage premium in the unionized sector x

P_x = the price of industry x's product

P_y = the price of industry y's product

w = wage rate in the y industry (hence, w(1 + Z) is the wage rate in the x industry)

FL = labor's share of total cost

FK = capital's share of total cost

We can use the rental price of capital services as the numeraire in expressing product and factor prices. Hence, the rental price of capital would then be 1 and $\frac{dr}{r} = 0$. Consequently,

$$\frac{dP_x}{P_x} - \frac{dP_y}{P_y} = FL_x \left(\frac{dw}{w} + dZ\right) - FL_y \left(\frac{dw}{w}\right) \tag{6-40}$$

The demand schedule for the x product would then be:

$$\frac{dq_x}{q_x} = E \left[FL_x \left(\frac{dw}{w} + dZ\right) - FL_y \left(\frac{dw}{w}\right) \right] \tag{6-41}$$

The supply schedule of product x is:

$$\frac{dq_x}{q_x} = FL_x \frac{dL_x}{L_x} + FK_x \frac{dK_x}{K_x} \tag{6-42}$$

The elasticities of factor substitution are:

$$S_x \left(\frac{dw}{w} + dZ\right) = \frac{dL_x}{L_x} - \frac{dK_x}{K_x} \tag{6-43}$$

$$S_y \left(\frac{dw}{w}\right) = \frac{dL_y}{L_y} - \frac{dK_y}{K_y} \tag{6-44}$$

Since $dK_y + dK_x = 0$, and $dL_y + dL_x = 0$, then:

$$S_y \left(\frac{dw}{w}\right) = - \frac{L_x}{L_y} \frac{dL_x}{L_x} + \frac{K_x}{K_y} \frac{dK_x}{K_x} \tag{6-45}$$

Equating 6–41 and 6–42, we have:

$$E \, FL_x \, dZ = E \, (FL_y - FL_x) \frac{dw}{w} + FL_x \frac{dL_x}{L_x} + FK_x \frac{dK_x}{K_x} \tag{6-46}$$

We can use Cramer's rule to reach the solution of equations 6–43, 6–45, and 6–46:

$$\frac{\frac{dw}{w}}{dZ} = \frac{E \, FL_x \left(\frac{K_x}{K_y} - \frac{L_x}{L_y}\right) - S_x \left(FL_x \frac{K_x}{K_y} + FK_x \frac{L_x}{L_y}\right)}{E \, (FL_y - FL_x) \left(\frac{K_x}{K_y} - \frac{L_x}{L_y}\right) + S_x \left(FL_x \frac{K_x}{K_y} + FK_x \frac{L_x}{L_y}\right) + S_y} \tag{6-47}$$

When $FL_y - FL_x \gtreqless 0$, then $\frac{K_x}{K_y} - \frac{L_x}{L_y} \gtreqless 0$. Consequently, $(FL_y - FL_x)(\frac{K_x}{K_y} - \frac{L_x}{L_y}) \geq 0$. In order for an increase in the wage premium to raise wages in the y industry, the unionized industry x must be capital intensive.

Similarly, we can solve equations 6–43, 6–44, and 6–45 to obtain the relative employment effects of union wage differentials:

$$\frac{\frac{dL_x}{L_x}}{dZ} = \frac{E(FL_y S_y \frac{K_x}{K_y}) + S_y(E \cdot FL_x + S_x FK_x)}{E(FL_y - FL_x)(\frac{K_x}{K_y} - \frac{L_x}{L_y}) + S_x(FL_x \frac{K_x}{K_y} + FK_x \frac{L_x}{L_y}) + S_y} \quad (6\text{--}48)$$

Since the denominator of equation 6–48 is negative and the numerator is positive, the relative employment effect must be negative.

VII. MINIMUM WAGE RATES, COLLECTIVE BARGAINING AND SOUTHERN INDUSTRIAL DEVELOPMENT

Government minimum wage legislation also raises wage rates and destroys potential employment in the covered industries. Unskilled labor will have fewer employment possibilities if the minimum wage level is above the competitive level of wages for their particular skill, although those who manage to stay employed will earn higher wages. Employers, faced with rising wages for unskilled labor, will usually try to substitute more highly skilled labor and capital for the unskilled. This implies that skilled labor will benefit from minimum wage legislation even though they were already earning wages above the minimum level. It is no surprise that organized labor is so interested in higher minimum wage rates and extended coverage.

Henry Simons [7] and John Van Sickle [8] interpreted the minimum wage legislation (especially in the 1930s and 40s) as a re-

---

7. Henry Simons, "Some Reflections on Syndicalism," in *Economic Policy for a Free Society*, Chicago: University of Chicago Press, 1948.

8. John Van Sickle, "Geographic Aspects of a Minimum Wage," *Harvard Business Review*, Spring, 1946.

flection of the political interests of a Northern coalition of industrialists and labor organizations. One of the greatest inducements for industry to move to the Southeast has been the possibility of hiring Southern workers at lower wage rates than those prevailing in the North. It is in the interest of labor and management in Northern industries to prohibit workers from being hired at lower wages in the South. This point was brought out very clearly by Senator Jacob Javits of New York:

> I point to Senators from industrial states like my own that a minimum wage increase would also give industry in our states some measure of protection as we have too long suffered from the unfair competition based on substandard wages and other labor conditions in effect in certain areas of the country—particularly in the South.[9]

Federal minimum wage legislation brought Southern wage rates more into line with those paid in the North, but the acts requiring industry-wide collective bargaining were the most effective in eliminating the North-South wage differential in industries important to the North. The National Industrial Recovery Act established industry-wide bargaining in the bituminous coal industry. Under these collective bargaining arrangements, the United Mine Workers succeeded in eliminating the North-South wage differential in 1941. The UMW was supported, of course, by Northern mine operators.

The elimination of the North-South wage differential by industry-wide collective bargaining and federal minimum wage legislation benefitted the Southern workers who enjoyed the privilege of employment at the higher wage rates. However, the situation was tragic for the Southern rural poor whose exodus from the failing agricultural sector was thwarted by the retarded growth of Southern industry. These wage policies (minimum wage and industry-wide collective bargaining) prevented the growth of Southern industry which could have competed with its Northern counterparts, and trapped many Southern workers in the low income agricultural sector which was not covered by the minimum wage.

When discussing wage differentials, it is important to distinguish between differences within a community and differ-

---

9. *The Congressional Record*, February 23, 1966, p. 2692.

ences within an industry. Within a community, wage differentials for similar types of labor must result from some labor monopoly. Obviously, such wage differences would induce low wage labor to transfer to the high wage sector. To sustain such wage differences, barriers must be created to restrict employment in the high wage areas. The most common barriers are minimum wage policies which have been legislated or agreed to in collective bargaining negotiations which prevent employers in the high wage sector from hiring willing and qualified workers at wages below the existing wage rate. When firms in the high wage sector are forced to pay wage rates above the prevailing rate in the community by minimum wage legislation or collective bargaining negotiations, the incentive to expand output and employment is destroyed. Obviously, it is not in the interest of the poorest workers in the community to have wage rates maintained at a high level relative to prevailing wages in the high productivity sector because the maintenance of the wage differential destroys alternative job opportunities.

Wage differentials between communities may also be eliminated by the migration of labor from the low wage regions to the high wage regions. Indeed, substantial migration from the South to the North has occurred since the 1930s. For most individuals, however, that migration was a painful experience. Because of the high cost of such migration, unusually large wage differentials are often necessary to induce substantial labor migration, particularly between regions where there are cultural differences.

Fortunately the wage differentials can be eliminated without the costs of labor migration through the flow of capital into low wage regions. The profit incentive resulting from wage differentials reduces the need for labor migration. However, if the inter-industry wage differentials are eliminated by collective bargaining or legislated minimum wages, the incentive for capital to move to the low wage regions is destroyed. Those industries whose wage bill for unskilled labor represents the largest proportion of total costs will have the most incentive to move to the South, if lower wage rates are allowed to prevail in that area.

A. MONOPSONY

There is one situation in which effective minimum wage legislation will not reduce potential employment of the unskilled. This is the case of the nondiscriminating monopsonist, made famous by Joan Robinson and Paul Douglass. An employer acts as a monopsonist if he faces a distinctly upward-sloping supply curve of labor. Since a nondiscriminatory monopsonist must pay all of his workers the same wage rate, anytime he raises wages to attract a new employee he must increase everyone's wages. The marginal cost of labor consists of the additional wages paid to the new employee plus the increment in the wages paid to all existing employees. The monopsonist will stop hiring new employees where the marginal revenue product of labor is equal to the total increase in labor costs necessary to hire an additional employee—his wage rate plus the increment in wages paid to all existing employees. The monopsonist's marginal labor cost (MLC) is:

$$\frac{dC}{dN} = w + \frac{dw}{dN} N$$

$$= w \left(1 + \frac{dw}{dN} \frac{N}{W}\right)$$

$$= w \left(1 + \frac{1}{\varepsilon_1}\right) \qquad (6\text{--}49)$$

where C = total costs

N = number of workers employed

w = wage rate

ε_1 = wage elasticity of the supply of labor

It is possible for minimum wage legislation to simultaneously raise wage rates and lower the marginal cost of labor because the elasticity of the supply of labor is infinite in the region where the minimum wage is effective. If the costs of hiring additional workers fall because of the minimum wage, the nondiscriminatory monopsonist will have an incentive to hire more labor. Figure 6–3 shows the marginal revenue of labor schedule, the

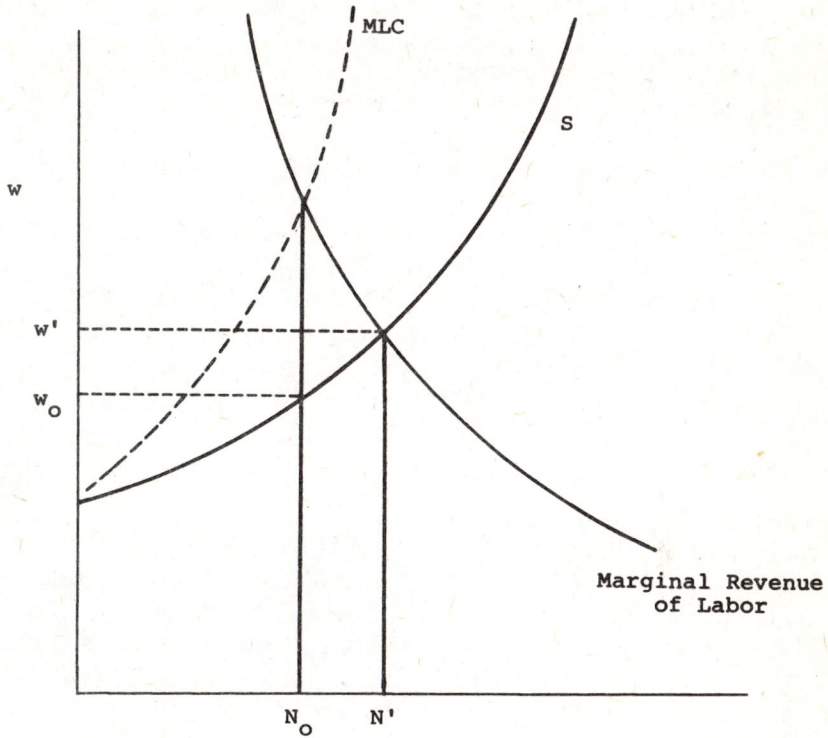

Figure 6-3

Minimum Wage Imposed on Nondiscriminating Monopsonist

labor supply schedule, and the marginal cost of labor schedule as functions of employment. The nondiscriminating monopsonist would hire N_o workers and pay them a wage w_o. If a minimum wage of w' is imposed on the employer, he will increase his labor force to N' because the supply of labor becomes infinitely elastic at w'.

This argument is seldom taken seriously, however. There are few situations where employers face distinctly rising supply curves of unskilled labor. Moreover, even if there were monopsonists, they could probably devise a scheme to confine the higher wage rate to marginal employees without having to raise the wages of their existing labor force.

One simple test of the relevance of the nondiscriminating monopsonist analysis to a particular situation is to observe whether there are qualified and willing workers who cannot get a job at the current wage rate. The validity of the nondiscriminating monopsony analysis rests on the assumption that wage rates must be raised to attract additional workers and those wage increases must also be paid to the existing labor force. If there are qualified workers who desire employment at the current wage rate, the elasticity of the supply schedule of labor is infinite.

VIII. AGGREGATE DEMAND AND LABOR MARKET RESTRICTION

The most careful and complete analysis of the unions' impact on inter-industry wages appears in *Unionism and Relative Wages in the United States* by H. Gregg Lewis. Lewis estimated the average union wage to be 10 to 15% above the average nonunion wage for workers of comparable skill and occupation in the period 1957–58. This wage differential was as high as 25% or more in the period 1931–33, but fell to less than 5% during the period 1945–49. The post-war disequilibrium wage differential can be attributed to the rapid growth in union membership which took place during the wartime wage controls and to the relative wage rigidity of union wages during the immediate post-war demand inflation.

In a later study, A. W. Throop provided additional evidence in support of Lewis' estimates.[10] Throop estimated the increase in the union-nonunion wage differential to be 12.5 percentage points during the period 1950–60.

Typically, the wage differential has increased during periods of unanticipated demand deflation and decreased during periods of unanticipated demand inflation. This phenomenon has been noted by a number of economists, including Albert Rees,[11] Milton Friedman,[12] and H. G. Lewis.[13] The cost of negotiating collective bargaining agreements usually discourages frequent contract renegotiations. As a result of the longer duration of col-

---

10. A. W. Throop, "The Union-Nonunion Wage Differential and Cost-Push Inflation," *AER*, volume LVIII, no. 1 (March, 1968).

11. Albert E. Rees, "Post-War Wage Determination in the Basic Steel Industry," *AER*, volume XLI, no. 3 (June 1951), pp. 395–399.

12. Milton Friedman, "Some Comments on the Significance of Labor Unions for Economic Policy," in David McCord Wright, ed., *The Impact of the Union* (New York: Harcourt, Brace and Co.), 1951.

13. H. G. Lewis, *Unionism and Relative Wages in the United States* (Chicago), 1963.

lective bargaining agreements, adjustments to unanticipated changes in aggregate demand are slower in the union sector of the labor market. More recently, Ashenfelter, Johnson and Pencavel concluded:

> . . . the evidence from the period since 1954 suggests that the pressure of trade unionism has been a major factor in the insulation of a large part of the manufacturing work force's wages from the short-run influences of market forces. This implies that sustained short-run market forces are likely to have an influence on wage changes only after prolonged time periods.[14]

H. G. Lewis also has estimated the relative employment effects of the union-nonunion wage differential.[15] Lewis estimates the elasticity of demand for union labor to be about −1.25 for man-hours and −0.74 for employees. These estimates imply that the 13 percentage point increase in the union-nonunion wage differential during the 1950s reduced potential employment in the unionized sector by about 9.6% and potential man-hours by 16%.

The reduction of relative employment in the unionized sector resulting from an increase in the union-nonunion wage differential contributes to national unemployment in the short run. The transfer of labor from the organized to the unorganized sectors of the labor market will usually require some period of search unemployment during which workers seek alternative employment opportunities. Moreover, A. C. Harberger, although specifically analyzing the effects of minimum wage legislation in Panama, argues that the steady-state unemployment equilibrium may be positively related to the steady-state wage differential between the protected and unprotected sectors of the labor market.[16] In the protected sectors paying wage premiums, individuals will be willing to bear higher search costs of unemployment to obtain employment. The higher search costs of obtaining jobs in the protected sectors reflected in longer durations of unemployment are offset by the wage premiums obtained

---

14. Ashenfelter, Johnson, and Pencavel, *Review of Economic Studies*, volume XXIX, no. 117 (January, 1972), p. 47, 1971.

15. H. G. Lewis, "Efficiency in the Labor Market: Relative Employment Effects of Unionism," *AER*, volume LIV, no. 3 (May, 1964).

16. A. C. Harberger, "On Measuring the Social Opportunity Cost of Labour," *International Labor Review*, volume 103, no. 6 (June 1971), pp. 559–579.

by eventual employment. The increase in the return to search unemployment resulting from the existence of a steady-state wage differential between the protected and unprotected sectors of the labor market increases steady-state unemployment.

As we have previously mentioned, the longer duration of collective bargaining agreements causes adjustments to unanticipated changes in aggregate nominal demand to be slower in the unionized sector of the labor market. Consequently, an unanticipated inflation results in greater relative employment in the unionized sectors of the economy. This has led some policymakers to advocate expansionary demand policies to reduce labor market imperfections caused by legislated and union minimum wage restrictions. Of course, unions could hedge against unanticipated changes in aggregate nominal demand with purchasing power contracts. However, cost-of-living escalators have played a relatively minor role in collective bargaining agreements. During the period 1964–67, only about two million workers were covered by cost-of-living escalators. The level of coverage did, however, increase to 4.3 million workers in 1972 after the experience with accelerating inflation from 1967–1971. This still only represents less than one-fourth of the unionized labor force. It seems plausible that if the rate of inflation continues to fluctuate widely, this trend will continue.

CHAPTER 7. WAGE AND PRICE CONTROLS

Most economists agree that long-run price movements are determined principally by government monetary and fiscal policies. Unfortunately, monetary and fiscal restraint has never successfully reduced inflation in the past without causing a recession. If the growth of nominal aggregate demand is reduced, prices and wage offers will rise at a slower rate than previously expected. Economic decisions during the adjustment period will be based upon expectations of the higher rate of wage and price inflation. Union leaders will seek higher wages to protect workers' earnings from continued inflation. Business firms will expect to meet these wage demands through price increases. Since the expected rate of inflation is not consistent with full employment at the slower rate of growth of nominal aggregate demand, labor contracts based on those inflationary expectations will result in sub-optimal employment in the unionized sector of the economy. In the nonunionized sector, where wages are contracted for shorter periods of time than in the unionized sector, nominal wage offers will rise at a slower rate as the growth in nominal aggregate demand slows. The gap that develops between actual wage offers and expected wage offers induces unemployed individuals to reject current wage offers and remain unemployed in the expectation of receiving higher offers. The unemployed will overinvest in the search for higher wages, increasing the average duration of unemployment. During this period of adjustment to a lower rate of inflation, unemployment in the past has temporarily increased for perhaps two or three years because of the gap between actual wage and price levels and their expected levels.

Although wage and price controls cannot be effective in situations of demand-pull inflation, they may be effective in reducing inflationary expectations which are producing cost-push inflation in an economy with a large unemployed stock of manpower and other resources. If wage and price controls are successful in speeding the adjustment of inflationary expectations to a lower rate of inflation, the adverse employment effects may be avoided. This argument for controls assumes a disequilibrium situation where widespread unemployment makes additional supply possible. By reducing inflationary expectations, wage and price controls shift the short-run Phillips curve downward, dissipating the inflationary pressures produced by labor costs without producing shortages.

In competitive labor markets where arbitrary wage floors do not limit job vacancies, all workers can obtain jobs at wages which make their employment profitable to the firm. If controls reduce prices, a continued supply of job vacancies will require lower wages. Lower wages, though, usually reduce the supply of labor unless workers' wage aspirations fall proportionally. To prevent shortages, wage and price controls must induce workers to accept job offers at lower wage rates. Unemployed workers reject job offers if they anticipate receiving higher wage rates. If wage and price controls psychologically discourage workers from holding out for better wages by reducing their expectations, controls may succeed without producing shortages.

Similarly, where labor unions have established wage premiums which limit job vacancies, there are qualified workers who cannot obtain jobs. If wage controls reduce union wages to the competitive level, employment and output will expand. The lower wage rates will make it profitable for employers to hire more workers. Since there is already excess supply of labor (scarcity of vacancies and abundance of job applicants), a fall in wages will result in more employment, increasing output and making lower prices possible without shortages.

I. EXPECTATIONS

We have already referred to the possibility of using direct wage and price controls in an attempt to manipulate aggregate supply conditions—i. e., to prevent the aggregate supply schedule from rising as rapidly as it otherwise would have. The essential channel through which wage and price controls may have their desired effect on aggregate supply conditions is through their effect on inflationary expectations. Remember, we postulated several models of expectations formulation in Chapter 5. The most widely posited one uses an adaptive expectations approach; past rates of inflation are the key to formulating expectations about the future. Another possibility considered that individuals' current information on other exogenous variables, i. e., monetary and fiscal policies, is used to predict future rates of inflation.

In the context of wage and price controls, however, economic agents may respond to legislated controls by drastically reducing the importance placed on past exogenous series. Some economists have pointed to evidence supporting this possibility. After the imposition of Nixon's Phase I freeze in 1971, market long-term interest rates fell significantly. According to the Fisherian proposition that inflation expectations are reflected in the level of nominal interest rates, one could view the above mentioned fall in long-term interest rates as supporting the proposition that expectations of future inflation fell drastically. Of course, on the other hand, interest rates (both short-term and long) rose dramatically during the 60 day freeze on prices during the summer of 1973. The evidence, then, does not support any consistent effect of direct controls on inflationary expectations.

The conclusion we draw is that controls can have only limited success in manipulating expectations. Consumers and businessmen may be mistaken occasionally about the future course of inflation, but ultimately they respond rationally to economic reality. Moreover, even if controls do succeed in influencing expectations, their success may produce a conditioned response which produces adverse effects on inflationary expectations when controls are removed. In addition, the possibility of future controls may actually be inflationary, as producers raise prices in anticipation of future price freezes even though current market conditions do not warrant such increases.

II. AGGREGATE EXCESS DEMAND SITUATIONS

Obviously, wage and price controls cannot be used as a substitute for monetary and fiscal restraint in the reduction of demand-pull inflationary pressures. If the government's monetary and fiscal policies produce a rapid increase in the rate of growth of nominal aggregate demand, price controls cannot prevent inflation without creating shortages. When wage and price controls hold the prices of products below uncontrolled market prices in competitive markets, prices send false signals about production and consumption. Lower prices motivate consumers to demand more, while profit maximization motivates producers to reduce the quantity supplied at lower prices. The resulting excess demand will create shortages.

A. MACRO CONSIDERATIONS

Aggregate excess demand for goods and services is caused by the private sector's attempt to spend more than their receipts in an attempt to get rid of excess money balances. If price controls prevent monetary equilibrium from being reestablished at a higher price level, the excess demand for goods and services will create shortages.

Widespread shortages destroy the usefulness of money balances as a medium of exchange. In the extreme situation, individuals will refuse to accept money in payment for labor services if they cannot use those money balances to buy goods. Eventually the economy will resort to barter or the use of a commodity currency which is free from price controls. Widespread shortages resulting from price controls in Germany after World War II induced the Germans to use cigarettes and cognac as the medium of exchange.

Even when no excess demand for goods and services exists, there is the danger that controls could stifle economic recovery if profit margins are kept too low. Producers are interested in maximizing their profits. As long as the increased costs of hiring additional employees are less than the increased revenue their employment generates, producers will find it profitable to expand output and increase employment. A freeze on profits would destroy the incentive for business to expand output and employment. It would be extremely naive to depend upon business charity to provide new jobs. In late 1970, the Canadians abandoned their wage and price controls because the policies of labor-dominated boards lowered profit margins excessively. This situation contributed to the 6.6% unemployment rate in Canada at that time.

B. MICRO CONSIDERATIONS

Even without aggregate excess demand, controls prevent *relative* prices from responding to market forces. This creates shortages in specific industries without causing short-run aggregate excess demand which could destroy the use of fiduciary money as a medium of exchange.

Consider the example in Figure 7–1. SS represents the ag-

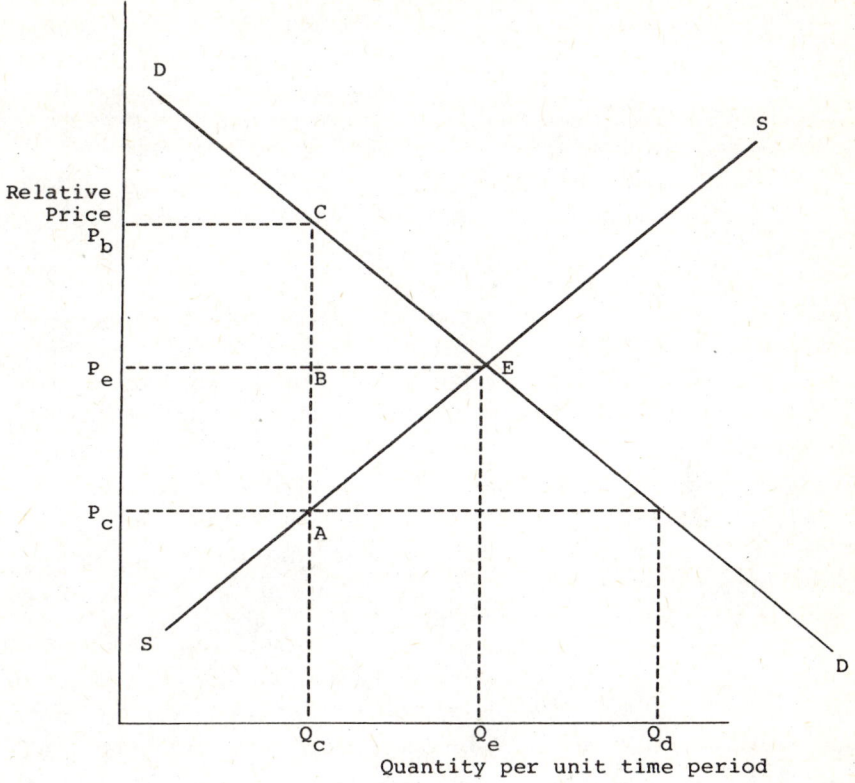

Figure 7-1

gregate supply schedule for an industry of price-takers. DD represents the consumers' marginal evaluation of the economic value of varying quantities of output (measured in constant quality units). We assume in this analysis that any income redistribution which results from direct wage and price controls has no effect on the DD schedule. Without controls, equilibrium is established with relative price P_e and quantity Q_e. A lower price, P_c, is legislated. At P_c manufacturers will be induced to provide Q_c while consumers will demand Q_d. The distance $Q_d Q_c$ represents unsatisfied demand. The rectangle $P_c ABP_e$ represents a transfer of producers' to consumers' surplus resulting from the lower price paid for Q_c units of output under the price control scheme.

The economic welfare losses depend critically on the system by which output is distributed among consumers. If efficient black markets operate, the economic value of output at the margin will be the same for all consumers. Consequently, the area $Q_c CEQ_e$ can be interpreted as the economic value to consumers of the output which is no longer produced because the price ceiling discourages production. If marginal cost equals price in other sectors of the economy, the area under the supply schedule $Q_c AEQ_e$ can be interpreted as the economic value of other goods sacrificed by using resources to supply the output $Q_c Q_e$ because the market value of marginal resources used in increasing output reflects the value of their marginal product in other sectors of the economy.* ACE is a net welfare loss to society resulting from the price ceiling. This welfare loss means that the economic losses to those who are harmed by the price ceiling exceed the economic gains to those who benefit. Since ACE represents a net welfare loss, the price ceiling would never be politically feasible if compensation were made to those individuals who are harmed. Under majority rule, however, such an economically inefficient rationing scheme may be feasible since the majority coalition may consist of the net beneficiaries.

Moreover, if black markets are not efficient, the net economic welfare loss will exceed ACE. Since the economic value of output at the margin may not be the same for all consumers, all the gains from voluntary exchange among consumers will not be realized. For example, consider Figures 7-2 and 7-3. Consumer A gets $\overline{X}_A$ units of output at the rationed price P_c, while consumer B gets $\overline{X}_B$. If there are efficient black markets, consumer A would sell $\overline{X}_A - X_A^o$ on the black market, and consumer B would purchase $X_B^o - \overline{X}_B$. The shaded triangles represent the economic gains to each consumer realized from exchanges on the black market. If efficient black markets are suppressed by the government, the gains from exchange between consumers represented by the shaded areas will not be realized. Consequently, the net welfare loss will exceed ACE.

---

* If monopoly power or taxes distort prices so that they no longer reflect the marginal rate of transformation between goods, this analysis of welfare losses breaks down because the market value of marginal resources no longer reflects the value of their marginal product in other sectors of the economy. In such situations, any statement about welfare losses or gains must specifically consider the sectors to which resources are transferred.

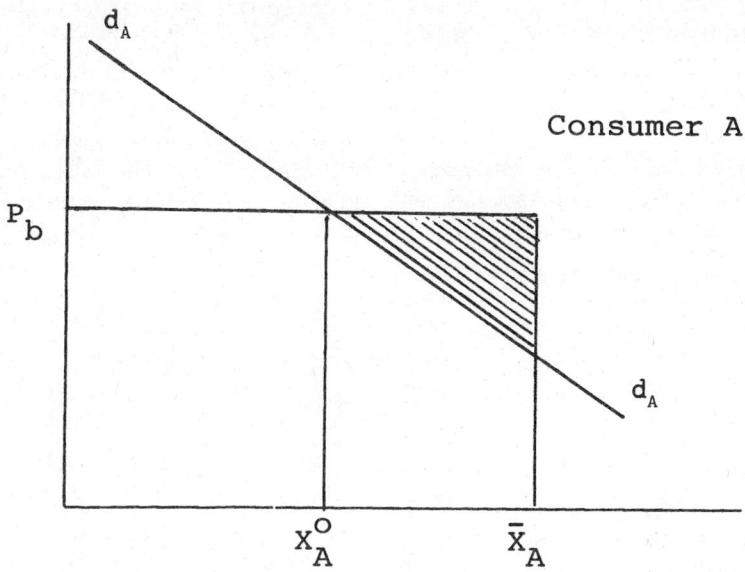

Figure 7-2

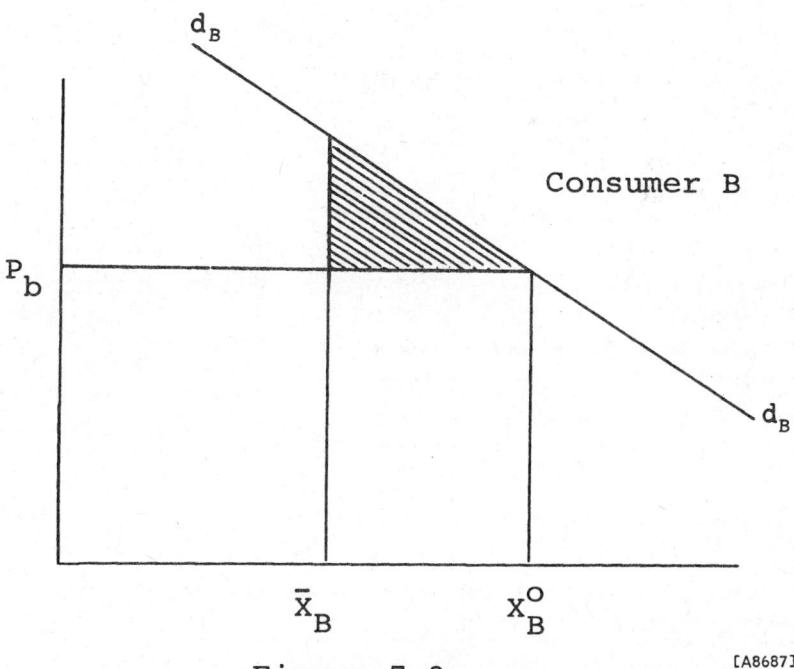

Figure 7-3

When price controls create shortages which are not rationed through black markets, some buyers prefer to pay higher prices rather than do without additional consumption. Those buyers who cannot obtain the goods in short supply at the official ceiling price will form coalitions with sellers, who obviously prefer higher prices. The greater the excess demand for goods and services, the larger the proportion of buyers who will join sellers in coalitions to raise prices.

C. INVENTORIES

When the possibility of future widespread shortages threatens to destroy the direct control system, the apparent market shortages will increase due to speculative hoarding of inventories by both producers and consumers. The possibility of higher future prices after controls are lifted constitutes an anticipated return to inventory investment which induces an increase in speculative stocks for any given nominal rate of interest. However, the demand for loanable funds to finance such inventory speculation raises market rates of interest. The return to speculative inventory accumulation is profitable only when the expected rate of inflation over the storage period is greater than or equal to the nominal interest cost of inventory financing plus storage costs (expressed as a percentage of the purchase price). Rapidly rising market interest rates typically characterize the breakdown of price control programs. The rise in short-term interest rates during the summer of 1973 may be interpreted as the anticipation of the price bulge following the end of the 60 day price freeze.

III. PRICE SEARCHERS MARKET

Some proponents of permanent wage-price controls (most notably John Kenneth Galbraith) base their support on the belief that giant corporations and labor unions have considerable market power and use that power to restrict output in order to get higher prices for the goods and services they sell. This popular economic argument is also used to justify permanent price fixing by regulatory commissions.

Firms with market power have negatively sloped demand schedules for their output. No firm can sell more output unless it lowers the price at which output is sold. Consequently, marginal revenue is the price at which one additional unit of output can be sold minus the loss of revenue from selling the rest of the output at a lower price. The profit maximizing firm will produce where marginal cost equals marginal revenue:

$$\text{marginal revenue} = (P + \frac{\Delta P}{\Delta Q} Q) = P (1 + \frac{1}{\eta}) \qquad (7\text{-}1)$$

where P = price

Q = quantity sold

η = elasticity of the demand schedule

If price ceilings are fixed, the demand schedule will become perfectly elastic in the region where the price ceiling becomes effective. In that region restricting output will no longer raise prices because of the controls. Price controls could raise marginal revenue while decreasing the price level. Since producers have an incentive to expand output when marginal revenue exceeds marginal cost, price ceilings above marginal cost may simultaneously reduce prices and provide an incentive to increase employment and output.

This argument for price ceilings on firms facing negatively sloped demand curves for their output pertains to relative prices, not necessarily absolute prices. If price ceilings cause price-makers to expand output, resources are absorbed which may reduce output and raise prices in other sectors of the economy. Absolute prices would fall only if the additional resources necessary to expand output were initially unemployed.

Even though price ceilings on price-makers may not reduce absolute prices in the economy, the expansion in output by price making firms may improve the allocation of resources. For instance, consider Figure 7–4. The price-making firm represent-

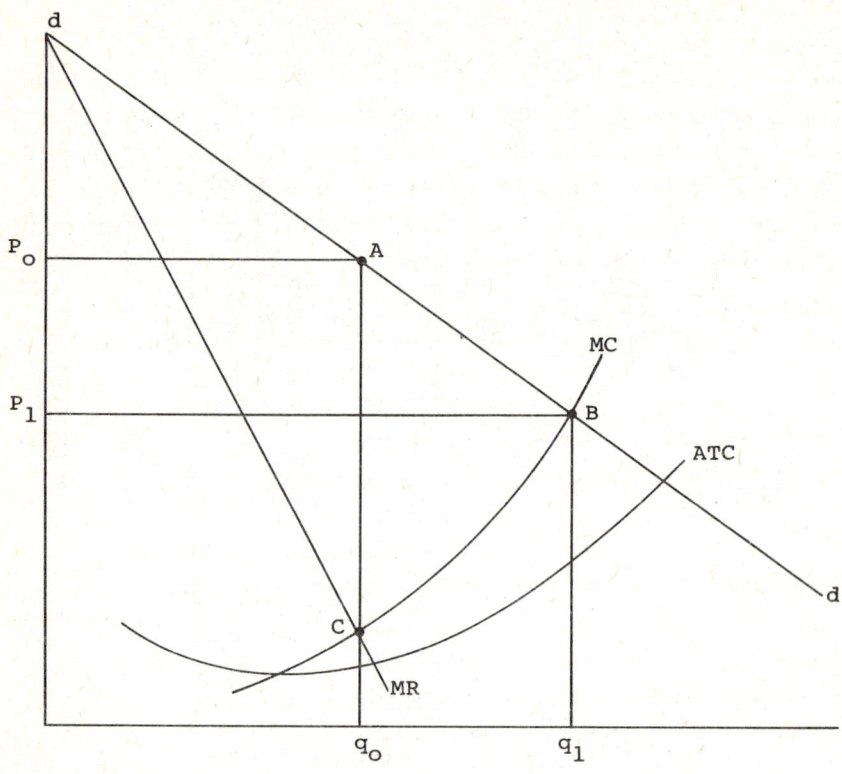

Figure 7-4

MR = marginal revenue

MC = marginal cost

ATC = average total cost per unit

dd = demand curve for the firm's output

ed in Figure 7-4 would maximize its profits by producing q_0 units of output and selling it for P_0 per unit if it had to sell all units of output for the same price. A price ceiling at P_1 would induce the firm to expand output to q_1. The area $q_0 ABq_1$ is the economic value of the additional output $q_1 - q_0$ to consumers. If all other sectors of the economy were marginal cost pricing, the area $q_0 CBq_1$ would measure the economic value of other goods sacrificed in order to acquire the additional resources necessary to produce $q_1 - q_0$. Consequently, the area ABC is a net welfare gain. This welfare analysis, of course, depends critically on the assumption that all other sectors of the economy are marginal cost pricing. If the market value of the marginal resources necessary to produce the additional output $q_1 - q_0$ does not equal the value of their marginal product in other uses, the analysis breaks down. If price distortions are already present, any analysis of welfare gains or losses necessitates specific knowledge of the sectors to which resources are transferred.

Price ceilings on price making firms also reduce the firm's incentive to incur demand increasing selling costs (such as advertising). If price is greater than marginal cost because the firm faces a downward sloping demand schedule for its output, the firm has an incentive to incur selling costs which increase demand at a given price to the point where the cost of increasing demand one more unit is equal to price minus marginal cost. If price ceilings induce the firm to marginal cost price, the firm will eliminate demand increasing selling costs. This effect on selling costs increases the possibility that price ceilings on price making firms will not produce shortages, for they simultaneously shift the demand schedule to the left as advertising and other selling costs are reduced. However, consumers may regard the reduction in the firm's selling costs as a loss of net welfare. Many selling costs, for instance, make shopping more convenient and efficient. In the absence of advertising expenditures by firms, consumers may have to use their own resources in generating information previously provided by firms. Consequently, the reduction in demand increasing selling costs may be regarded as a reduction in the quality of the product.

Many firms facing negatively sloped demand schedules do not earn excessive profits. Since price controls reduce the quasirents earned by the owners of sunk investments, they may still reduce output in the long run even though they may temporarily increase output in the short run. For instance, consider Figure 7–5. A price ceiling at P_1 will increase output to q_1 in the

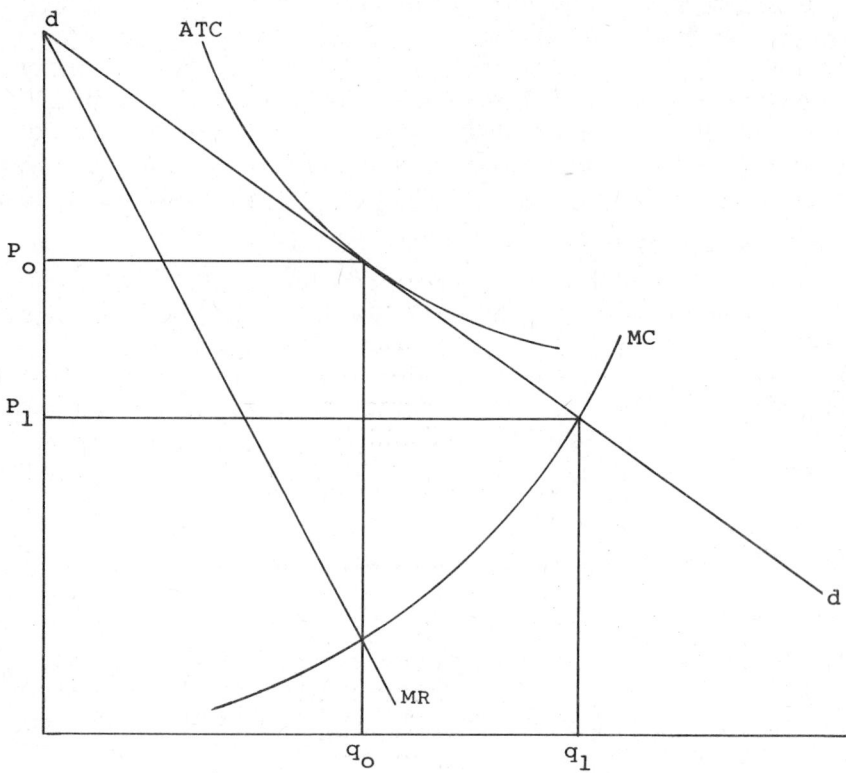

Figure 7-5

short run. In the long run, however, the firm will go out of business because P_1 is less than average total cost (ATC).

IV. FIXED AND VARIABLE COST CONSIDERATIONS

Many industries have required relatively large sunk capital cost outlays. Hence, quasi-rents exist in these industries. In the short run, most of the reduction in producer surplus resulting from price controls will be borne by the owners of those factors of production which are in relatively inelastic supply. It would seem that price control programs can exploit the owners of sunk investments in the short run.

However, in the long run additional investment is necessary to maintain or increase supply. Such an investment will occur only when the marginal revenue stream produced by the additional investment is sufficiently high to be profitable.

The existence of quasi-rents makes it possible for labor to transfer most of the reduction in producer surplus to the owners of sunk investments. Such income transfers cannot, however, be long-lived, for the reduction in capital investment will eventually reduce output capacity. Thus, short-run reduction in prices due to direct controls tends to have pernicious long-run effects in output supplied. That is, the long-run supply schedule is far more elastic than the short-run supply schedule.

Hence, even though direct controls may reduce inflation without serious rationing problems, in the long run the reduction in investment may lead to a future price level higher than it would have been (at any given wage rate) had controls never been attempted. For the lower future capital stock implies lower future productivity, and *ceteris paribus*, a higher price level (for a given wage rate).

V. EFFECTS OF ALTERNATIVE CONTROL SCHEMES

A centralized bureaucracy cannot easily serve as a substitute for the price system, which provides information about changes in consumer demands and incentives to efficiently satisfy those demands. Prices must respond to changes in costs in order to insure production adequate to prevent shortages. In the attempt to sustain profit margins under changing cost conditions, price regulators have, of necessity, adopted rules which allow producers to raise prices when confronted with cost increases. Cost-plus or profit margin rules provide that sort of flexibility for the price controls. Unfortunately, those arbitrary rules which allow firms to charge cost plus a percentage of cost reduce the incentive to produce economically and efficiently. Moreover, cost-plus rules may induce the producer to inflate costs artificially in order to raise prices.

In the absence of price controls, price-making firms will produce where marginal revenue equals marginal cost. This requires the firm to produce in the region where the demand schedule is elastic. However, when a firm receives a fixed portion of total revenue, as would be the case under the cost-plus rule, the profit-maximizing firm will produce where the elasticity of demand is -1 (where total revenue is maximized). This will usually require lower prices than would be needed in the absence of controls. To the extent that profit margin rules reduce the incentive to produce efficiently, though, such rules contribute to inflation rather than prevent it. When firms produce inefficiently they absorb resources which could increase output elsewhere and thus raise prices in other sectors of the economy.

Profit margin controls may also discourage investment in labor-saving equipment. Such investment could increase aggregate output per worker and thus reduce inflationary pressures from the cost side. A firm finds it profitable to purchase relatively expensive labor-saving equipment only if that investment increases profit margins, for increased profits are necessary to provide an adequate rate of return on the new investment.

Profit margin rules are clearly inappropriate where increased demand can be satisfied only by the entry of high-cost producers into the industry. Profit margins of the low-cost producers must rise in response to market forces. Prices must rise to levels which make the entry of high-cost producers profitable.

Similarly, productivity increases are sometimes used as one of the criteria for permissible wage increases in order to provide flexibility in controlled wages. Indeed, growth in aggregate output per man-hour for the whole economy does define the rate of wage increase that is noninflationary. The reason is that labor's share of total income is fairly constant, consequently the ratio of prices to unit labor costs should be fairly constant in the long run. The increase in unit labor costs is the percentage increase in wage rates minus the percentage increase in output per man-hour. Consequently, if wages increase at 5.5% per year and output per man-hour increases at 3% per year, prices should increase at only 2.5% per year in the long run.

For an individual industry, however, this criterion is inappropriate. Within an industry substantial increases in output per man-hour may be achieved by substituting labor-saving equipment for workers. Such automation is usually the result of increasing wage rates. When the competitive wage rate increases and causes automation, automation is socially desirable because in other sectors of the economy workers can earn wage rates higher than the wage rate required to prevent automation. However, where wage rates are artificially increased by union power or government legislation, automation unemploys workers who cannot receive wage rates elsewhere which are higher than the wage rate which would make automation unprofitable. It is economically absurd to suppose that increases in output per man-hour resulting from automation brought on by higher wage rates are a justification for additional wage increases. The increase in output per man-hour in an industry which automates in response to wage increases in excess of those that would have occurred in a competitive labor market does not usually increase aggregate output per man-hour. The automation, which would not have occurred in the absence of union power, requires the absorption of savings which could have increased output per man-hour in other sectors of the economy.

VI. CONCLUSIONS

Although many alternative control schemes could and have been devised, the general conclusion from our last section will probably still apply: control schemes may negatively influence productivity and, hence, reduce the rate of growth of labor's real wages. Moreover, for any given level of nominal wage, the reduction in productivity, referred to in both sections IV and V, alone will, *ceteris paribus,* raise long-run prices above the levels that would have existed in the absence of controls.

There are many grave risks associated with wage and price controls which seem to outweigh their presumed benefits. The most serious danger is that the controls will be used as a substitute for responsible monetary and fiscal policies which would prevent inflation from occurring in the first place. Ultimately the government's monetary and fiscal policies will determine the rate of inflation. If the aggregate nominal demand growth rates are excessive, wage and price controls cannot effectively halt inflation; they can only create shortages. When the controls are lifted, inflation will return.

CHAPTER 8. POLICY–MAKING IN THE POST–NEW ECONOMIC ERA

In previous chapters we have discussed the possibilities of using aggregate demand policies to control the unemployment rate. In the process, we emphasized the essential presumption that biased expectations are fundamental to any trade-off between inflation and unemployment. Policy-makers have "control" of the unemployment rate only when future price movements are predictable only by the policy-makers themselves, and not by the economic agents. The assumption of rationality, however, appears to destroy any presumption of policy-makers being in such a position. If policy-makers use any specific model of expectations formation to derive the forecasts of the economic agents, such models will predict only so long as policy-makers continue to act in such a way as to create private unbiased forecasts. As soon as policy-makers use the model to create consistently biased forecasts, rational individuals will soon correct their models to yield unbiased forecasts.

The policy-maker's dilemma is, therefore, that the use of any knowledge of disequilibrium price dynamics to manipulate the voluntary behavior of economic agents in such a way as to be detrimental to their self-interest (even though it may be socially desirable) will cause rational individuals to modify their behavior, nullifying the presumed "economic" law.

The apparent success during the 1960s of the "New Economists" use of expansionary demand policies resulted principally from the period of extreme price stability during the previous decade. Economic agents had grown accustomed to relatively stable price levels. In such a situation, the expected rate of return to accurately forecasting the future rate of change in aggregate inflation was small compared to the return to forecasting movements in relative prices. Increases in aggregate demand could produce significant increases in employment because expectations of aggregate inflation were slow in changing.

The expected return to learning about the determination of the rate of inflation depends upon recent history of the variability in the rate of inflation. Hence, the accelerating inflation from 1965 to 1970 provided large incentives to correct decision rules to reflect higher future rates of inflation. As a result, policy-makers soon were faced with the "apparent" paradox of an inflationary recession.

Furthermore, the recent variability in the actual rate of inflation has induced economic agents to invest considerable resources in forecasting the future rate of inflation. When monetary and fiscal policies are widely variable, the returns to predicting the future rate of inflation in terms of sophisticated models increases. Adjustment lags estimated from past economic series will prove useless for policy making purposes. The recent variability of monetary and fiscal policies has induced individuals to make their forecasts determined to a great extent by recent developments in aggregate demand policies. These arguments lead us to the conclusion that the employment effects of aggregate demand policies should be significantly less than in the past. Changes in aggregate nominal demand will have larger short-run effects on prices and less on output.

Furthermore, the increased variability in demand policies will induce contracts which minimize the importance of predicting the future rate of inflation. For instance, collective bargaining agreements which embody cost of living escalator clauses have increased as a result of the difficulty in accurately predicting future inflation.

Even the most basic of policy-makers' goals, the unemployment rate, seems open to serious criticism. Recent models of voluntary unemployment, such as that presented in chapter 3, cast doubt on the advisability of using any numerical target as full employment goal. In the absence of any model which can accurately predict the amount of voluntary unemployment consistent with unbiased forecasts by the economic agents, the use of any specific unemployment rate target is likely to produce undesirable fluctuations in the rate of inflation.

There is no stable law of disequilibrium dynamics. The implications of this statement for aggregate demand employment policies should, by now, be obvious.

*

INDEX

References are to Pages

A

Accelerationists and Phillips Curve, 58
Allais, Maurice, 63
Arrow, K. J., 61
Ashenfelter, Johnson, and Pencavel, 89n.

B

Balancing leakages, 12
Black markets, 96
Bowen, William G., 47
Brimer, Roger, 51

C

Cagen, P., 60
Cambridge equation, 12
Capital services, 71
Cobb-Douglas, 21
Cost, unit labor, 22

D

Demand, nominal, 5
　for labor, 19, 69
Demand and supply of labor, 19, 23
Douglass, Paul, 86

E

Eckstein, Otto, 51
Employment effect, 68
Expectations:
　and inflation, 30
　and unemployment, 50
　changing expectations, 56
　formation of, 60

F

Fisher, Irving, 59
Friedman, Milton, 44, 58n., 60, 63, 88
Friedman interpretation of the Phillips Curve, 44

G

Gordon, Donald, 49
Gould, J. P., 63
Government:
　budget constraint, 7
　policy maker's dilemma, 48

H

Hamilton, M. T., 49
Harberger, A. C., 89
Hicks, J. R., 15
Hoarding, 6
　and dishoarding in government, 7
Holt, Charles C., 30
Hynes, J. A., 49

I

Inflation,
　cost-push, 25
　demand-pull, 24
　　theories, 25
　unanticipated, 2
　weaknesses of demand-pull and cost-push, 26
Inflationary taxation, 8
Information and job search, 30
Interest rates in IS–LM, 16
Inventories, 98
IS–LM curves, 15

J

Javits, Jacob, 84
Johnson, Harry G., 80

K

Keynes, J. M., 8n., 11, 59
Koyck, L. M., 60

INDEX

L

Labor market:
  Demand, 19, 69
    derivation, 73
    empirical examples, 77
    general equilibrium considerations, 80
    market restrictions and, 65, 88
  Supply, 19
Lewis, H. Gregg, 75, 88, 89n.
Lucas, Robert, 64

M

Mieszkowski, P., 80
Mills, E. S., 61
Minimum wage: see Wages, minimum
Money, high powered, 9
Money creation, 10
Money supply: determinants, 9
Monopsony, 86
Muth, John, 62, 64

N

National Bituminous Coal Wage Agreement, 76
Nelson, C. R., 63
Nerlove, M., 61
Nominal demand: see Demand, nominal

O

Okun, Arthur, 26n.
Okun's Law, 26

P

Phelps, E. S., 49
Phillips, A. W., 2, 46
Phillips curve, 2, 46
  and expectations, 54
  and changing expectations, 56
President's Council of Economic Advisors, 65
Price searchers market and wage-price controls, 98
Probability density function of wage offers, 31
  variance of, 38
Production function: Cobb Douglas, 21

R

Random walk model, 63
Rees, A. R., 49, 49n., 88n.

Reservation wage rate, 31
Robinson, Joan, 86

S

Samuelson, Paul A., 2, 46
Scale effect, 71
Schwartz, Anna, 63
Simons, Henry, 83, 83n.
Solow, Robert, 2, 46, 46n.
Spencer, Roger, 51

T

Taxation, by inflation, 8
Throop, A. W., 88

U

Unemployment:
  wage rigidity and, 28
  voluntary, 30
  search, 29
  duration, 34
  in planned economies, 36
  errors in forecasting, 40
  and inflation trade-off, 2, 46; see also Okun's Law
  inflationary expectations and, 50
Unions
  and unionization rates, 66
  collective bargaining, 67
United Mine Workers, 75, 84
UMW v. Pennington, 76

V

Van Sickle, John, 83, 83n.
Velocity of Money, 14

W

Wages:
  aggregate excess demand, 93
  and price controls, 65, 91
  and price controls: welfare effects, 94
    effects of alternative control schemes, 103
    effect of expectations, 92
    fixed and variable cost considerations, 102
    price searchers market, 98
  differentials: welfare effects, 78
  minimum, 83
  minimum wage in Panama, 89
  reservation wage rate, 31
Wagner Act, 44
Williamson, Oliver, 76n.

END OF VOLUME